THERMAL CONDITIONS IN FREEZING LAKES AND RIVERS

THERMAL CONDITIONS IN FREEZING LAKES AND RIVERS

A. A. Pivovarov

Translated from Russian by E. Vilim
Translation edited by P. Greenberg

A HALSTED PRESS BOOK

JOHN WILEY & SONS
New York · Toronto

ISRAEL PROGRAM FOR SCIENTIFIC TRANSLATIONS
Jerusalem · London

Sole distributors for the Western Hemisphere and Japan

HALSTED PRESS, a division of
JOHN WILEY & SONS, INC., NEW YORK

Library of Congress Cataloging in Publication Data

Pivovarov, Anatoliĭ Aleksandrovich.
Thermal conditions in freezing lakes and rivers.

"A Halsted Press book."
Translation of *Termika zamerzaîushchikh vodoemov.*
1. Lakes – Temperature. 2. Rivers – Temperature.
3. Ice on rivers, harbors, etc. I. Title.
GB1605 .P5813 551.55′248 73–12269
ISBN 0–470–69103–4

Distributors for the U.K., Europe, Africa and
the Middle East

JOHN WILEY & SONS, LTD., CHICHESTER

Distributed in the rest of the world by

KETER PUBLISHING HOUSE JERUSALEM LTD.

ISBN 0 7065 1350 9
IPST cat. no. 22075
UDC 551.48 + 551.46

This book is a translation from Russian of
TERMIKA ZAMERZAYUSHCHIKH VODOEMOV
Izdatel'stvo Moskovskogo Universiteta
Moscow, 1972

Printed in Israel

Contents

This monograph provides a generalized physicomathematical description of the formation of the temperature regime and ice phenomena in shallow water bodies (storage lakes, lakes, rivers). Topics treated include calculations of the main heat balance components, spring and summer heating and fall cooling of waters, the temperature regime of ice-covered lakes and rivers in winter, the buildup and thawing of the ice cover and the winter dynamics of ice phenomena in open sections of water. Theoretical methods are improved, and standard working formulas suitable for practical application are presented and tested against observation data.

The book is intended for a broad range of specialists engaged in the investigation and calculation of temperature and ice regimes of storage lakes and rivers. It may also serve as a textbook for postgraduate and undergraduate students specializing in geophysical and hydrological subjects.

INTRODUCTION

If natural water bodies are to be used rationally, detailed and comprehensive information must be available on the main elements of their regime in different seasons. The associated problems are very varied. The processes are complicated and require further study.

The present monograph confines itself to examining problems connected with the formation of the thermal regime of water bodies liable to freeze over (chiefly lakes and storage lakes) in the annual cycle of its changes. In the case of such water bodies it is usual to divide the year into the summer period, when the water surface is free of ice, and the ice period, which commences when compact pack ice forms on the surface of the water and ends with its clearance. Intermediate periods are the freezing period in fall and the disintegration of the ice in spring, characterized by the existence of discrete masses of frazil and surface ice. Such a division is physically justified by the different factors that determine the fundamental regularities governing the formation of the temperature field in water and of ice phenomena in lakes and rivers.

The thermal conditions of lakes and rivers are determined by the absorption of radiant energy of the sun, heat exchange with the atmosphere and the bottom, and the redistribution of heat in the water via transport by currents and turbulent mixing. Experimental investigations into the thermal conditions of lakes and rivers must therefore encompass a broad range of measurements of basic actinometric, meteorological and hydrological elements for determining the heat balance components and the turbulent heat transfer in water and in the marine surface layer.* There are as yet few such measurements, especially in the open parts of storage lakes and lakes, and measurements of turbulence are very sparse.

A full treatment of the forecasting of the thermal regime of lakes and rivers must include a quantitative description as dependent on the physical conditions and extraneous factors. Owing to energy exchange at the interfaces the temperature distribution in the water is closely related to the thermal and dynamic regime of the marine surface layer and the thermal conditions of the bottom. Hence it is

* [This is the lowest atmospheric layer over the surface of any water body, not only of seas and oceans.]

necessary to examine simultaneously the formation of the main meteorological and hydrological elements in all interacting media.

The greatest difficulties in stating and solving the general problem are caused by insufficient knowledge and complexity of turbulent exchange processes in the atmosphere and in the water. Random fluctuations in the instantaneous values of wind and current speeds, water and air temperatures and of other elements of the hydrodynamic fields with different time and space scales cause an abrupt increase in the processes of transfer of impulse, heat, and other properties in comparison with molecular processes. A full description of such pulsating fields can only be statistical with certain probabilistic conclusions relating to some mean characteristics.

Quantitative descriptions and practical calculations of averaged fields are still based on semiempirical theories using various hypotheses concerning coefficients of turbulent exchange. This yields a closed system of equations. However, the exchange coefficients thus introduced depend on the kinematic structure and properties of the turbulent flow. The establishment of these relations is one of the main problems of the dynamics and thermal conditions of lakes and rivers and has not yet been solved.

The condition of quasi-steady fluxes of momentum, heat and moisture in the marine surface layer is generally included in the statement of the problem in hydrophysical investigations. In this way the transfer equations for the atmosphere and the lake or river can be treated separately. When the problem is thus posed, the dynamic and thermal effect of the atmosphere is calculated by the heat balance equation at the water — air interface. This creates certain limitations as to the methods of predicting the water temperature, because the initial data assumed in the marine surface layer depend on the thermodynamic conditions of the lake or river. This limitation is immaterial only for the ice period, because then the decisive factors are the hydrological conditions and the heat exchange with the bottom or with deep waters.

The most important morphological characteristic in the formation of the thermal conditions of lakes and rivers is the depth. In this respect all water bodies can be divided into two groups: shallow bodies with large water surface area, in which turbulent exchange affects the water down to the bottom; and deep bodies characterized by a thermocline separating surface waters from deep waters. Here the depth of the surface or active layer is not constant but is determined by the entire complex of physical conditions. The calculation of the position and thickness of this layer is one of the fundamental problems of the dynamics and thermal conditions of deep water bodies.

The most advanced theory deals with calculation of the temperature field in the ice-free period and its prediction in the presence of a contiguous ice cover on the water. However, even in these cases the calculation methods are not completely closed, because it is necessary to know preliminarily the coefficient of turbulent heat exchange in the water, and this in turn depends on the stratification of the temperature. For nonsteady problems (which are of greatest interest when dealing with thermal conditions of freezing lakes and rivers) the question of closing the equations of turbulent transfer requires special investigation. Any progress in its solution is bound up with an examination of the general theory of turbulence and practical applications in lakes and rivers.

If the coefficients of turbulent exchange are known, existing methods make it possible to calculate the temperature field in the water fairly reliably for the ice-free period as regards thermal interaction with the atmosphere. When there is a compact pack ice cover it can be predicted for the entire ice period from the known initial conditions in the previous summer. Knowledge of the water temperature beneath the ice cover also permits one to solve fairly completely the problem of the buildup or thawing of the ice from below. Less well-known are problems of the thermal conditions and ice phenomena in the periods of fall freezing and spring clearing of ice. So far no sufficiently general and reliable quantitative theory exists for these processes which would yield results satisfying practical requirements.

In practical applications the most widely used methods are those establishing empirical relations and heat balance methods which yield integral, statistically averaged characteristics of the individual elements of the thermal regime under actual conditions as dependent on factors that are extraneous to the water body. There is ample literature that deals with these aspects. The present author did not set himself the task of providing a detailed survey of such investigations, which are mostly of a regional nature.

This book concentrates mainly on the possibility of a general physicomathematical description of the formation of different stages of the thermal regime of water bodies in the annual cycle of its changes. Investigations in this field began to develop quite recently; their number is small and no generalizations have been made. Monographs dealing with the study of individual heat balance components for the ice-free period and with the thermal regime in winter do not fully describe annual changes in the thermal conditions of freezing lakes and rivers. In this connection the generalization of existing investigations is timely with a view to the further development of reliable quantitative techniques for calculating and forecasting the annual course of the thermal and ice regimes of freezing lakes and rivers.

The first chapter deals with methods of calculating the different heat balance components and is largely an introduction that requires further exposition. The second and third chapters contain a generalization of the investigations to the formation and calculation of the temperature field in water for the ice-free period and of the thermal regime in winter. The fourth and final chapter examines problems of the dynamics of ice phenomena connected with the existence of frazil and of sections that do not freeze over. In this way the full cycle of annual changes in the thermal conditions of freezing lakes and rivers is treated.

The monograph draws heavily on studies conducted by the author and staff of the Department of Physics of the Sea and Inland Waters of the Physics Faculty of Moscow State University. Some of this work forms the main content of some chapters of this book.

The author is greatly indebted to A. G. Kolesnikov, Member of the Academy of Sciences of the Ukrainian SSR, who headed the first investigations into the thermal conditions of seas and storage lakes, Academician V. V. Shuleikin for a number of valuable hints, Professor A. M. Gusev and Professor A. G. Sveshnikov for detailed revision of the manuscript, and to all those who took part in the work.

Chapter I

HEAT BALANCE COMPONENTS OF LAKES AND RIVERS

§1. THE HEAT BALANCE EQUATION

The formation of thermal processes in water is determined by the absorption of radiant energy from the sun, by energy exchange at the interfaces with the atmosphere and the bottom, and also by heat redistribution in the water as a result of convection by currents and turbulent mixing of the water masses. The complex interdependence of these factors gives rise to a temperature field which is nonuniform in space and nonsteady in time, but involves phase transformations and other thermal phenomena in the water. So far a quantitative description of the main regularities governing the formation of thermal conditions in lakes and rivers is possible only by accepting certain schematic simplifications of the actual interaction of the decisive factors and hydrological conditions in different seasons of the year.

The general thermal state of water masses is described by the heat balance equation, which expresses the law of conservation and conversion of energy. This equation can be written for the lake or river as a whole, or for some part of it. When a temperature field in water is described with allowance for turbulent mixing, the heat balance is compiled for infinitesimal elements of volume and time, which leads to the differential equation of heat transfer.

The main sources contributing to heating of the water are: absorption by water of the total radiant energy from the sun, intake of heat from the atmosphere as a result of turbulent exchange and condensation of water vapor, influx of heat from the bottom and via warm currents. Heat expenditure and water cooling occur as a result of effective emission by the water surface, evaporation, heat emission to the atmosphere, the bottom, and via cold currents. If ice phenomena exist on lakes or rivers, heat exchange during freezing of the water and thawing of the ice is essential to the heat balance.

In addition, a number of less important or incidental heat sources and sinks are present, such as increase of heat owing to dissipation of the kinetic energy of currents, heat exchange during chemical and biological processes, heat exchange associated with precipitation. The quantitative role of these factors is slight compared with the main components.

Consider a water column of unit cross-section and height h (from the surface of the water body to its bottom). The simultaneous action of the main heat sources and sinks at the boundaries and inside the considered volume determines the time variation in enthalpy. This is expressed analytically by the heat balance equation

$$c\rho h \frac{\partial \bar{t}}{\partial \tau} = (1 - A) I_0 - R \pm P \pm lW \pm Q_b \pm Q_c \pm Q_i, \qquad (1.1)$$

where c, ρ and $\bar{t}$ are specific heat, density, and vertically averaged water temperature; I_0 is flux of total solar radiation; R is effective radiation by water surface; A is albedo of water; P and W are fluxes of heat and moisture in the marine surface layer;* l is evaporation temperature; Q_b is heat exchange with the bottom soil; Q_c and Q_i are heat exchanges when there are currents and ice phenomena; τ is time. Fluxes entering the volume in question are treated as positive, while fluxes emerging from the volume are negative.

The role and importance of the various components of this equation may differ, depending on the hydrometeorological conditions, and this permits some simplification in solving actual problems. For instance, in summer, when there are no ice phenomena and the currents are stable, the main features of the state of water bodies are determined by interaction with the atmosphere, described by the first four terms on the right-hand side of equation (1.1). In winter freezing of lakes and rivers, when the water surface is covered by compact pack ice, the thermal effect of the atmosphere influences mainly the buildup and thawing of the ice, and only slightly affects the water temperature. Changes in water temperature are determined mainly by heat exchange with the bottom and turbulent exchange in the water, so allowing one to make predictions for the entire ice period.

There is much literature dealing with the experimental determination and methods of calculating the principal heat balance components. The examination of these problems as applied to marine conditions was begun by Shuleikin /91/. His investigations have been used extensively in general climatological works /10, 82/, in heat balance calculations for different water bodies as a whole and for the vertically averaged water temperature, and

* [See footnote on p. 1.]

also for predicting the times of freezing and clearing of the water bodies /77/. In such calculations the heat balance components are determined by empirical formulas obtained for some mean conditions.

In recent years the heat balance method has been given new impetus by Timofeev /86/. A new feature is the use of the equations of heat and moisture exchange in the marine surface layer together with the heat balance equation pertaining to the active surface layer of the lake or river; and the equation of turbulent heat transfer in the water. Using some simplifying assumptions and hypotheses linking the vertically averaged water temperature with the surface temperature, Timofeev succeeded in obtaining a quite simple analytical solution for calculating the water surface temperature as a function of the main actinometric and meteorological elements. The actual results of these investigations are examined in more detail in the respective chapters.

Heat balance equation (1.1) and analytical expressions for the main components yield on the right-hand side the change in enthalpy for the entire volume under consideration. These integral balance methods are therefore insufficient without additional information and the predicted temperature field in the water. The solution of such problems involves the equations of turbulent transfer with corresponding boundary and initial conditions. In this connection we examine the heat balance equation pertaining to the water — air interface of the water body as this is one of the main boundary conditions in hydrophysical problems of heat transfer in water.

Before deriving the heat balance equation for the water surface, we add a few remarks about the absorption of radiant energy by water. Its attenuation depends largely on its wavelength and on the transparency of the water. Under actual conditions of lakes and rivers the attenuation factor of the total radiant energy flux changes from hundredths to tens per meter. In water with low transparency, for which the attenuation factor is large, the radiant energy flux is almost fully absorbed by a thin surface layer of the order of centimeters or decimeters. In water with high transparency the radiant energy penetrates to a considerable depth and gives rise to the appearance of vertically distributed heat sources.

The heat balance equation for the water surface is then easily derived from (1.1) by letting $h \to 0$. If in addition it is assumed that the value of $\frac{\partial t}{\partial \tau}$ is finite, we obtain two forms of the heat balance equation: if we assume that the radiant energy is completely absorbed at the surface (water with low transparency),

$$Q_w = (1 - A) I_0 - R \pm P \pm lW \tag{1.2}$$

and if we assume absorption of radiant energy in the bulk of the water (water with high transparency),

$$Q_w = -R \pm P \pm lW, \qquad (1.3)$$

where Q_w is the heat exchange in the water.

In investigations of the winter thermal regime the heat balance equation is expressed similarly, but its main components refer to the snow or ice cover.

§2. REFLECTION AND ABSORPTION OF RADIANT ENERGY

The first term in the right-hand part of heat balance equation (1.1) determines the amount of radiant energy penetrating the water, ice or snow cover:

$$Q_0 = (1 - A)\, I_0. \qquad (2.1)$$

Absorption and scatter in these media gradually attenuate the flux of radiant energy, which is finally transformed into heat. The change in flux (2.1) is determined by the laws governing changes in the total radiant energy flux reaching the surface, the albedo, and the physical properties of the media (water, ice, or snow).

A most comprehensive review of investigations into radiant energy fluxes and albedos of different underlying surfaces as dependent on various factors is given in monographs by Kondrat'ev /51, 53/ and Kirillova /37a/. Therefore we present here only information required for the further statement and solution of practical problems pertaining to the thermal conditions of lakes and rivers.

Upon reaching the water, ice or snow surface, part of the radiant energy flux is reflected and some penetrates the underlying medium. A certain fraction of the total flux scattered in this medium (backscattered radiation) returns to the atmosphere. The ratio between the total reflected and backscattered fluxes on the one hand, and the total incoming radiant energy flux determines the albedo of the underlying surface (water, ice, or snow). The experimental determination of this quantity by collectors, whose sensitivity is identical for any part of the spectrum of the incident and reflected radiant energy fluxes, yields the integral albedo for the entire spectrum. This quantity will be examined below.

The main factors determining the albedo are sun elevation, distribution and type of cloud cover, and state of reflecting surface. Greatest albedo variations are caused by direct solar radiation, since this depends mainly on sun elevation. With scattered radiation the albedo depends more on the distribution of brightness over the sky than on sun elevation. With respect to the total radiation the albedo is not obtained by adding its components; it depends substantially on the ratio of the fluxes of direct solar radiation and of scattered radiation.

The albedo for total radiation can be computed theoretically only if the distribution of brightness over the sky is known and the water surface is smooth, or if the water waviness is somewhat schematized /55, 64, 95, 96/. These calculations show that if the elevation of the sun is less than about 30°, the albedo of a wavy surface is smaller; at greater elevation it is more than the albedo of a smooth surface. These results agree with observation data.

When computing time variations in radiant energy fluxes penetrating the water it is desirable to have an analytical expression of the albedo as a function of sun elevation. Such expressions exist in exponential form /54, 76/. However, their application to theoretical calculations is inconvenient, because the elevation of the sun appears in the exponent.

Pivovarov et al. /73/ studied recorded radiant energy fluxes on the Black Sea and proposed a formula for calculating albedo in the case of clear sky and medium wave conditions (force 2 – 4):

$$A = \frac{a}{\sin h_{\odot} + a}, \tag{2.2}$$

where $a = 0.040$ is an empirical parameter and $h_{\odot}$ is sun elevation.

A comparison of (2.2) with observation data is presented in Figure 1 for the Black Sea and in Table 1 for two storage lakes, using data of Kirillova /37a/.

TABLE 1. Albedo of water for the total radiation as dependent on sun elevation

Data	Sun elevation, deg						
	5	15	25	35	45	55	65
Observation							
Volgograd Reservoir	26	13	9	8	6	6	5
Novosibirsk Reservoir	25	14	9	7	6	5	—
Calculation by formula (2.2) .	32	14	9	7	5	5	4

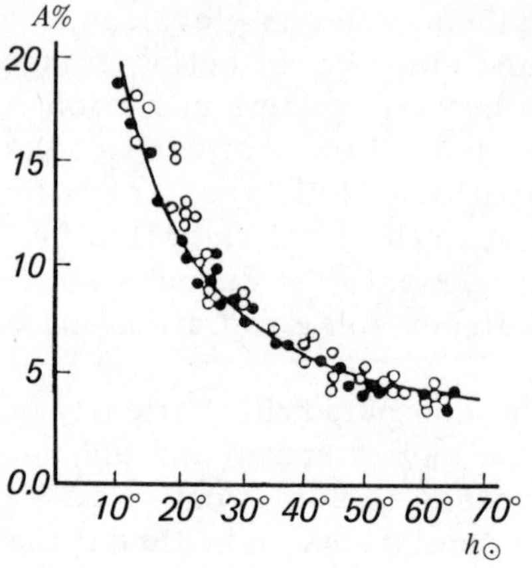

FIGURE 1. Albedo of water surface as a function of sun elevation: ——— by formula (2.2); ○,● — observation data.

Expression (2.2) agrees well with observation data and is sufficiently general for various water bodies with differing conditions. It can therefore be used to compute the albedo when direct measurements are lacking. Its advantage over exponential functions is that it can be more widely applied in theoretical calculations and that it contains only one empirical parameter.

If the elevation of the sun is small, expression (2.2) does not yield a maximum value of the albedo, as obtained by other theoretical calculations /64/ and some observations /53/, and the results are exaggeratedly high. On the other hand, when the sun elevation is small, the observations contain larger errors, the radiant energy flux is small and has no substantial effect on the thermal conditions in the water.

If we express the elevation of the sun as a function of the hour angle $\omega\tau$, the latitude of the place φ_C, and the declination of the sun δ_C by the relation

$$\sin h_\odot = \sin \varphi_C \sin \delta_C + \cos \varphi_C \cos \delta_C \cos \omega\tau, \tag{2.3}$$

then (2.2) yields the following diurnal course of the water albedo:

$$A = \frac{a}{a + B + C\cos\omega\tau}. \tag{2.4}$$

Quantities

$$B = \sin \varphi_C \sin \delta_C \quad \text{and} \quad C = \cos \varphi_C \cos \delta_C$$

in the course of a day for the given point may be considered constant. The time of rising and setting of the sun ($\pm\tau_0$) is determined by the condition sin $h_{\odot}=0$, which gives

$$\tau_0 = \frac{1}{\omega} \arccos\left(-\frac{B}{C}\right).$$

If we substitute in (2.4) various values of the hour angle in the time interval between sunrise and sunset, we obtain the full diurnal course of the albedo of the water body. Outside this interval the albedo is taken as zero.

When expression (2.4) is integrated with respect to time from $-\tau_0$ to τ_0 and then divided by $2\tau_0$, we obtain the mean diurnal albedo* in the form

$$A_{av} = \frac{a}{\omega\tau_0} F,$$

where

$$F = \begin{cases} \frac{2}{\sqrt{\Delta_1}} \operatorname{arctg} \sqrt{\Delta} & \text{for } \Delta_1 > 0, \\ \frac{1}{\sqrt{-\Delta_1}} \ln \frac{1+\sqrt{-\Delta}}{1-\sqrt{-\Delta}} & \text{for } \Delta_1 < 0, \end{cases}$$

$$\Delta_1 = (B+a)^2 - C^2;\quad \Delta = \frac{B+a-C}{B+a+C}\ \operatorname{tg}^2\left(\frac{\omega\tau_0}{2}\right).$$

Calculations of the mean diurnal albedo of the sea, calculated by these expressions /73/, agree well with results obtained with the aid of recorded data of radiant energy fluxes and with calculations using another method /85/. This agreement is an additional confirmation that (2.2) is correct.

Although the effect of waves, cloudiness, and water transparency on the albedo may be considerable, it nevertheless is in the nature of corrections and has not yet been described analytically. The corrections for waves, calculated by Ter-Markaryants from Caspian Sea observations, and by Kirillova /37a/ from observations at a number of storage lakes, are given in Table 2.

The quantitative character of the dependence of the correction for waves on the elevation of the sun is seen to be the same for seas and storage lakes: in both cases the smallest effect of the waves on

* Kirillova /37a/ in her monograph notes that the method of calculating A_{av} by this method is incorrect, but she is wrong.

the albedo is found at sun elevations of about 30°. Quantitatively, the correction for waves under storage lake conditions is smaller than at sea for all sun elevations.

TABLE 2. Dependence of correction $\Delta A = A_{st} - A_{wave}$ on sun elevation

$h_{\odot}$, deg		5	10	20	30	40	50	60
ΔA, %	sea	15	10	1.5	-1.0	-1.8	-2.5	-2.9
	storage lake	—	5	2.5	0.0	-0.5	-0.5	-0.5

Ter-Markaryants made allowance for the effects of waves, cloudiness, and mean transparency conditions and computed tables of the mean diurnal albedo of the sea for the total radiation at different latitudes and seasons of the year. The effect of cloudiness on the albedo is also minimal when the sun elevation is about 30°. Tables of conversion factors $A_{av}/A(h_{\odot})$, compiled by Kirillova /37a/, can also be used to rapidly estimate the mean diurnal albedo of storage lakes in the ice-free period.

The albedo of snow and ice fluctuates within broad limits mainly as a function of the state and structure of the snow and ice cover. The albedo of freshly fallen snow is close to 95 – 99%; the albedo of soiled and wet snow drops to 20%. The range of ice albedos is smaller, but still considerable. The albedo of pure ice is about 35 or 40%; the albedo of soiled melting ice drops to 10 or 15% /77/. Greatest fluctuations in the albedo of snow and ice covers occur during snowfall and during melting of snow and ice. So far it is impossible to quantitatively describe the full variability of the albedo of snow and ice as a function of different factors.

Consider briefly radiant energy flux variations at the surface of the earth. The main factors determining these changes are sun elevation, transparency of the atmosphere, degree and form of cloudiness, and the albedo of the surface. The flux of total radiation is much stabler than its components (direct solar radiation and scattered radiation). This considerably aids practical calculations.

So far the solution to the general problem of radiant energy propagation in the atmosphere does not yield effective practical results, because the absorption and scatter processes are so complicated. However, Berlyand's formula /3/ can be used as an approximate theoretical method of calculating the total radiation flux when the sky is cloudless:

$$I_0 = \frac{r^2}{r_0^2} \frac{S_0 \sin^2 h_{\odot}}{\sin h_{\odot} + (1 - A) f}, \qquad (2.5)$$

where $f=\alpha'\int_0^\infty \rho' dz$, S_0 is the solar constant, r_0 and r are the mean and instantaneous distances between earth and sun, ρ' is the density of atmospheric substances that attenuate radiation, α' is the scattering coefficient.

Berlyand's calculations show that coefficient f has a pronounced annual variation and geographical distribution. The values of this coefficient can easily be used to determine the radiant energy flux as a function of sun elevation; expression (2.3) yields the time dependence. Figure 2 shows that calculations by (2.5) agree fairly well with observation data /73/ for cloudless sky conditions. The value of parameter f is stable, and quantitatively it is close to its value for the given latitude and time of year. Similar agreement of (2.5) with observation data is also encountered in other papers.

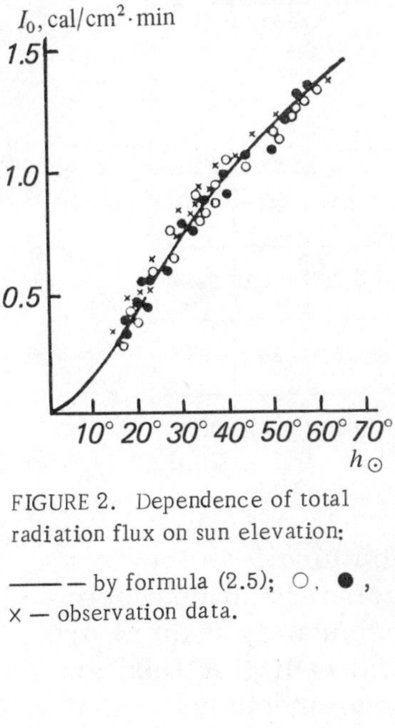

FIGURE 2. Dependence of total radiation flux on sun elevation:

——— by formula (2.5); ○, ●, × — observation data.

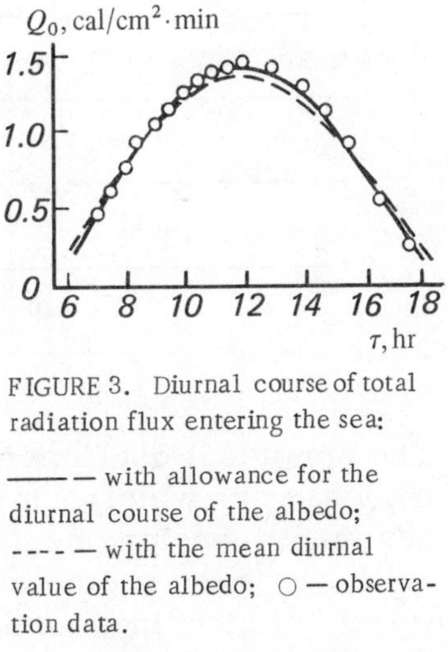

FIGURE 3. Diurnal course of total radiation flux entering the sea:

——— with allowance for the diurnal course of the albedo;

---- — with the mean diurnal value of the albedo; ○ — observation data.

Figure 3 compares measured radiant energy fluxes with values calculated by (2.1) with allowance for (2.5) and (2.2) and the mean diurnal value $A_{av}=0.074$, when $f=0.160$. As expected, if the dependence of the albedo on sun elevation is neglected, the calculated radiant energy fluxes are somewhat too low at high elevations and somewhat too high at low elevations (quantitatively these divergences are small, amounting to about 2% of the diurnal sums).

The effect of cloudiness on the total radiation flux is usually taken into account by introducing correction functions:

$$I = I_0 \begin{cases} f(N) = 1 - c_0 N, \\ f(N) = 1 - c_L N_L - c_M N_M - c_H N_H, \end{cases}$$

where N is the cloudiness in fractions, c_0, c_L, c_M, c_H are empirical coefficients expressing the effect of the total, lower, middle, and high clouds, respectively.

Berlyand studied extensive experimental material and proposed expressing the effect of cloudiness on the total radiation flux by a nonlinear correction function in the form

$$f(N) = 1 - (a_1 - b_1 N) N.$$

It was then ascertained that coefficient $b_1 = 0.38$ (constant) and that coefficient a_1 is a function of the latitude of the location. Its numerical values are given in Table 3.

TABLE 3

$h_{\odot}$, deg	0	5	10	15	20	25	30	35	40
a_1	0.38	0.40	0.40	0.39	0.37	0.35	0.36	0.38	0.38
$h_{\odot}$	45	50	55	60	65	70	75	80	85
a_1	0.38	0.40	0.41	0.36	0.25	0.18	0.16	0.15	0.14

The empirical coefficients in the correction functions for cloudiness vary widely. In calculations for actual locations their values must therefore be ascertained more accurately if there are any changes (even short-term ones) in the total radiation flux, and the forms of cloudiness must be observed simultaneously.

We shall examine the possibility of describing quantitatively the attenuation of the total radiant energy flux in water, ice and snow covers.

There are only few direct measurements of total radiant energy flux penetrating to different depths with the aid of receivers that are approximately equally sensitive over the entire spectrum. Analysis of these measurements shows that radiant energy penetrating water is most attenuated in the upper 1-m layer of water, and below this layer mostly visible rays penetrate. In water of low transparency the upper 2- or 3-m layer of water attenuates practically the entire flux of radiant energy penetrating beneath the surface.

There is a widespread belief that because of the strict selectivity of absorption and scattering the quantitative description of the attenuation of the total radiant energy flux in the water by the simple exponential law

$$Q(z, \tau) = (1 - A) I(\tau) e^{-\alpha z} = Q_0(\tau) e^{-\alpha z}$$

implies that attenuation factor α is dependent on sun elevation and the depth. The kind of dependence involved is shown in Figure 4 and in Tables 4 and 5, calculated from measurement results obtained in different lakes and rivers. The attenuation factor changes particularly rapidly in the upper water layers, where the bulk of infrared and red radiation is absorbed. As the transparency decreases, the attenuation factor increases and its variations become smaller with increasing depth.

TABLE 4. Attenuation factors (m^{-1}) by layers for total radiation*

Water body	Depth of layer, m					
	0—0.2	0.2—0.5	0.5—1.0	1—2	2—4	4—10
Lake Sevan	4.70	0.93	0.72	0.41	0.31	0.18
Kandalaksha Bay	3.13	1.23	0.84	0.58	0.33	—
Tsimlyanskoe Reservoir . .	2.23	2.21	2.03	2.08	—	—
Black Sea	2.2	—	0.46	—	0.32	—

* The chromaticity of water is given in units of the platinum-cobalt scale. "O" means that the water has no brownish or yellowish tinge. Organic silt content is given for the surface layers including centrifuged plankton and dissolved substances. Data for the calculations are taken from /31, 37a, 75/.

The selectivity of total radiant energy flux attenuation in water can be quite reliably and fully described by Kolesnikov's method /41/: the entire spectrum of the total flux is divided into different sections, some mean attenuation factor β_m is assumed for each section, and then the flux at any depth can be expressed in the form

$$Q(z, \tau) = Q_0(\tau) \sum_{m=1}^{\nu} I_m e^{-\beta_m z}. \tag{2.6}$$

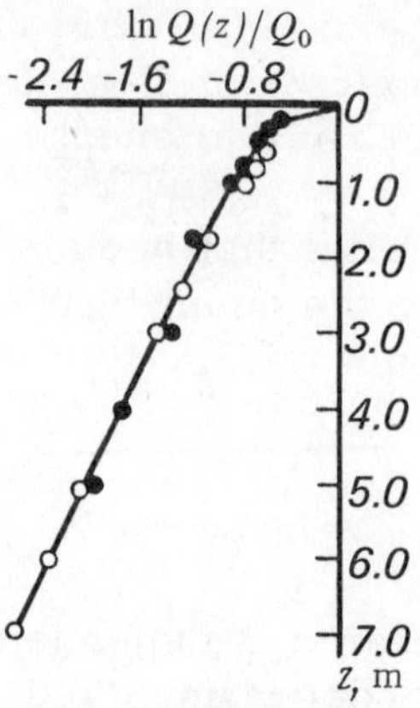

FIGURE 4. Changes in total radiation penetrating the water with increasing depth.

TABLE 5*

Lake	Depth of layer, m						
	0–1	1–2	2–5	5–9	Silt content, mg/l	Chromaticity of water	Depth at which white disk disappears
Little Bass . .	1.31	0.40	0.40	0.53	3.53	0	7.0
Pauto	1.51	0.38	0.41	0.32	4.44	0	8.3
Day	1.43	0.47	0.35	0.37	5.29	0	8.3
Silver	1.24	0.42	0.41	0.53	7.63	5	8.5
White-Sand .	1.39	0.45	0.42	0.72	8.81	12	3.1
Plum	1.66	0.64	0.68	0.62	10.69	16	4.9
Midge	1.77	0.84	0.54	0.68	10.54	20	4.2
Turtle	2.62	1.87	1.32		27.75	68	2.5
Little Long . .	2.75	1.83	1.19		31.51	96	2.0
Mary	3.54	1.95	1.10		38.86	132	1.7

* See Footnote to Table 4, p. 15.

Quantity $I_m = \frac{I_{m,\lambda}}{Q_0}$ can be taken as the relative spectral flux for section m of the spectrum.

Attenuation factors β_m and quantities I_m can be easily calculated numerically or graphically from measurements of the total flux of radiant energy at different depths /7, 75/. Such an analysis shows that under actual conditions it suffices to confine oneself to two or three terms of (2.6) to attain sufficient accuracy. There the attenuation factors β_m and relative spectral fluxes I_m for sun elevations exceeding 25 or 30° are practically independent of the elevation of the sun. This considerably simplifies the solution of problems on radiative heating of water masses.

Since at depths of more than one meter the penetrating solar radiation consists of visible light, the attenuation factors are somehow related to the depth at which a white disk disappears, characterizing the water transparency. The results of such a comparison are shown in Figure 5. The attenuation factor multiplied by the depth at which a white disk disappears is almost constant, equal to 2 in water with high transparency and 3.5 in water with low transparency. If the radiant flux is not measured at different depths, these relations can be used for approximate assessments of the attenuation factor in the visible region of the spectrum.

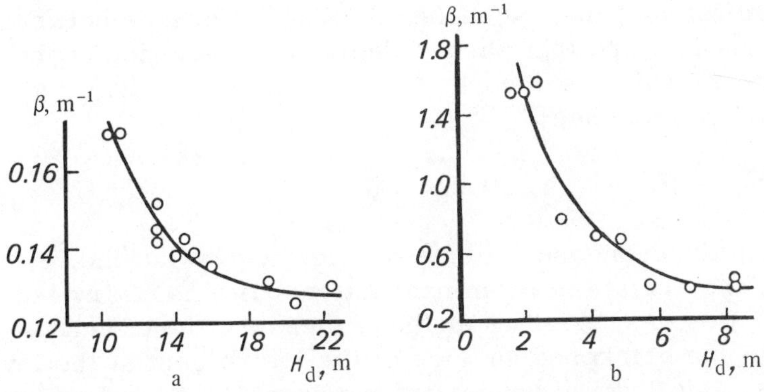

FIGURE 5. Relation between the attenuation factor of radiant flux in the visible region and depth H_d at which a white disk disappears:

a — sea /7/; b — lakes and storage lakes.

The quantitative description of the attenuation of total radiant flux in form (2.6) can also be used for its propagation in ice and snow covers. Then β_m and I_m are dependent on the state and structure of the ice or snow. Snow cover is most opaque to solar radiation. A 10-cm-thick snow layer almost completely absorbs the radiant energy of sun penetrating beneath the surface. This in particular is the reason why solar radiation has no effect on water temperature under ice and snow cover. Ice possesses higher transparency, and the penetration of total solar radiation through the ice cover and its absorption by the water causes a temperature maximum near the underside of the ice cover (cf. Chapter III).

§3. EFFECTIVE RADIATION AND RADIATION BALANCE

An underlying surface (water, ice or snow cover) as well as any heated body is a source of radiation whose flux obeys the Stefan–Boltzmann law

$$U = \delta\sigma T_n^4,$$

where $\sigma = 0.816 \cdot 10^{-10}$ cal/cm^2 · min · deg^4 is the Stefan–Boltzmann constant, δ is the relative radiating power, T_n is the absolute temperature of the radiating surface.

The atmosphere of the earth also yields a flux of thermal radiation, part of which is directed toward the surface of the earth (counterradiation of the atmosphere). The difference between the natural radiation, and that part of the counterradiation of the atmosphere δG which is absorbed by the surface is the effective radiation of this surface:

$$R = U - \delta G.$$

Although direct measurements of effective radiation are fairly numerous, they relate predominantly to conditions of dry land and nighttime. Besides, existing methods measure the effective radiation of the blackened surface of the instrument at the level where it is installed and not that of the underlying surface. If the pyrgeometric measurements are to yield true values of the effective radiation, a correction for the effective radiation of the air layer between the level of the instrument and the radiating surface must be introduced. With this correction, the effective radiation of the surface of water, ice, or snow assumes the form

$$R = \delta R_0 + \delta\sigma (T_n^4 - T_a^4), \qquad (3.1)$$

where R_0 is the effective radiation of the black surface of the pyrgeometer for air temperature T_a at the level where the measurements are taken, and T_n is the temperature of the radiating surface.

It is advantageous to simplify expression (3.1) somewhat by linearizing the second term. To this end we transform from absolute to centigrade temperatures by substituting $T_n = T_0 + t_n$ and $T_a = T_0 + t_a$ in the second term of (3.1). Expanding and omitting all terms of type $\frac{t_n + t_a}{T_0}$ raised to powers higher than the first, we obtain

$$R = \delta R_0 + 4\delta\sigma T_0^3 (t_n - t_a). \quad (3.2)$$

This expression will henceforth be used in problems dealing with thermal conditions.

The fundamental regularities of the effective radiation vs. time relationship are determined by the changes in the temperature of the underlying surface, the temperature and moisture distribution in the atmosphere, and the distribution over the sky and type of cloudiness. These laws are simplest for a cloudless sky.

Theoretical investigations /52/ and calculations show that the distribution of temperature and moisture in the atmosphere has a substantial influence on the effective radiation, and they are the physical substantiation for introducing a correction for the temperature difference between the underlying surface and the air at the level of effective radiation measurement. Introduction of this correction makes it possible to take into account the effect of the stratification of the atmosphere from surface data.

If there are no pyrgeometer measurements, R_0 is calculated by empirical formulas of general form

$$R_0 = \sigma T_a^4 f_1(e) f(N). \quad (3.3)$$

Function $f(N)$ expresses the effect of cloudiness on the effective radiation and is usually expressed in the form

$$f(N) = 1 - cN,$$

while function $f_1(e)$, which expresses the effect of atmospheric humidity, assumes the form

$$f_1(e) = \begin{cases} a_1' + b_1' \cdot 10^{-c_1' e}, \\ a_1'' + b_1'' \sqrt{e}. \end{cases}$$

Ångström proposed a power dependence of the effective radiation on atmospheric humidity in the correction function, and Brent proposed a dependence corresponding to the square root of the humidity. The latter is preferable, because it contains fewer empirical parameters.

The empirical coefficients in the correction functions for cloudiness and humidity of the air are mainly determined for dry land conditions, and they depend to a considerable extent on the latitude and time of year. The application of formulas like (3.3) may be justified when computing certain values of the effective radiation over sufficiently long periods of time.

Kirillova's measurement data /37a/ in a number of storage lakes under various conditions of cloudiness and temperature stratification in the marine surface layer led to the following formula for calculating the effective radiation of the water surface in the ice-free period:

$$R = 0.91\,\sigma T_a^4\,(0.41 - 0.05\sqrt{e})\,(1 - cN) + \\ + 0.0034\,(t_n - t_a) - 0.0065,$$

where e is atmospheric humidity in mb, $c = 0.61$ refers to cloudiness 10/10 (low) and $c = 0.39$ to cloudiness 10/0 (high).

The effective radiation of snow and ice cover can also be calculated by a formula of type (3.3) with corresponding coefficients in the correction functions.

The algebraic sum of the absorbed radiant flux and the effective radiation constitute the radiation balance of the surface or some active layer as a function of the transparency of the underlying medium. In media of low transparency the absorption of solar radiation can be assumed to occur practically only on the surface, and the radiation balance of the surface in that case is

$$B_r = (1 - A)\,I - R.$$

In media with high transparency this equation related to the active layer in which the radiant energy is fully absorbed. The radiation balance of such media in the surface layer is completely determined by the effective radiation.

The fundamental changes in radiation balance are naturally determined by changes in its individual components. However, time changes in the radiation balance proceed more smoothly. The most important daytime radiation balance component is the total solar radiation flux, and at night, the effective radiation.

For minor inland water bodies it is of interest that the radiation balance of the water may be determined from the radiation balance of the surrounding land. For deep and large water bodies the relation between the radiation balances of the dry land and of the water body itself is /37a/

$$B_r = B_1 + (1 - A)\,I - (1 - A_1)\,I_1 + G - \\ - G_1 - \delta U + \delta_1' U_1 - (1 - \delta)\,G + (1 - \delta_1')\,G_1. \qquad (3.4)$$

For small water bodies, where the difference between cloudiness over the water and over land and the differences in total radiation flux, counterradiation of the atmosphere, and between the radiating power of water and dry land may be neglected, expression (3.4) reduces to

$$B_r = B_1 + (A_1 - A) I + \delta\sigma (T_1^4 - T_n^4)$$

or approximately

$$B_r = B_1 + (A_1 - A) I + 4\delta\sigma T_0^3 (t_1 - t_n).$$

§4. TURBULENT HEAT AND MOISTURE EXCHANGE WITH THE ATMOSPHERE

Turbulent heat and moisture exchange with the atmosphere, which leads to heating or cooling of the underlying medium, is an important feature of the general interaction between the atmosphere and water. Many experimental and theoretical investigations deal with this interaction under different conditions. Their generalization for dry land conditions has been dealt with by Monin and Yaglom /63/ and Zilitinkevich /29/, for the ocean by Roll /79/ and Kitaigorodskii /37/, and for inland water bodies by Timofeev /86/.

We now examine the fundamental conclusions of such investigations concerning the possibility of describing quantitatively the turbulent fluxes of heat and moisture in the marine surface layer over water bodies in the ice-free period and over land or snow- and ice-covered water, and of calculating these fluxes from directly measured meteorological elements.

The surface or marine surface layer is usually understood to mean the air layer some tens of meters thick adjacent to the underlying surface. Its characteristic feature is the negligibly small influence of the Coriolis force on the statistical turbulence parameters and the constancy with height of the turbulent momentum, heat and moisture fluxes. The theoretical model of such a layer is the model of flow in a half-space over a plane surface with horizontally homogeneous parameters depending solely on the distance from the underlying surface.

If we mark by primes the instantaneous deviation s' of a variable from its mean value, the vertical turbulent flow F of some transferred property (momentum, quantity of heat or moisture) is

$$F = -\overline{(\rho w)' s'},$$

where w is the vertical component of wind speed, and the line indicates statistical averaging.

This expression shows that the direct determination of turbulent flows requires information on the instantaneous values of the variable fields and subsequent statistical averaging. To obtain them, highly sensitive, rapid-response apparatus and a corresponding recording method must be available. Such a method and apparatus are at present available for recording turbulent velocity and temperature fields. However not many such observations exist, and they concern mostly the ground layer over dry land. Direct measurements do not yet yield general laws governing turbulent flows and their relation to the averaged characteristics of variable fields.

Semiempirical theories of turbulence have found widespread application in solving practical problems. Exchange coefficient k enables the full vertical fluxes of momentum τ, heat P, and moisture W to be expressed in the form

$$\tau = \rho\nu_{\tau}\frac{du}{dz} + \rho k_{\tau}\frac{du}{dz}; \tag{4.1}$$

$$P = -c_p\rho\nu_t\frac{dt}{dz} - c_p\rho k_t\frac{dt}{dz}; \tag{4.2}$$

$$W = -\rho\nu_q\frac{dq}{dz} - \rho k_q\frac{dq}{dz}, \tag{4.3}$$

where c_p is the specific heat, q is the relative humidity of the air, u is the wind speed, t is the air temperature, ν_{τ}, ν_t, ν_q are the coefficients of molecular viscosity, thermal conductivity, and diffusion, respectively. The $0z$ axis points vertically upward from the underlying surface.

The coefficients of turbulent exchange, determined by $k = -\rho\overline{w's'}/\frac{ds}{dz}$ are not physical parameters like the coefficients of molecular thermal conductivity, viscosity, and diffusion; they depend on the scales and the kinematic structure of the turbulent flow. They can be expressed in terms of mean parameters by introducing additional assumptions concerning the nature of turbulent motion under certain conditions.

If the fluxes of momentum, heat and moisture are assumed to be quasi-steady, they can be expressed in terms of corresponding mean values of wind speed, temperature, and specific humidity at two levels. When (4.1), (4.2), and (4.3) are integrated with $\tau = \text{const}$, $P = \text{const}$, $W = \text{const}$, with respect to height from the underlying surface to some height h_0 in the air, we obtain

$$\tau = \rho C_u u^2 (h_0); \tag{4.4}$$

$$P = -c_p \rho C_t [t(0) - t(h_0)] u(h_0); \tag{4.5}$$

$$W = -\rho C_q [q(0) - q(h_0)] u(h_0), \tag{4.6}$$

where

$$C_s = \frac{-F_s}{\rho u(h_0)[s(0) - s(h_0)]} =$$

$$= \frac{1}{u(h_0)} \left[\int_0^{h_0} \frac{dz}{(\nu_s + k_s)} \right]^{-1}, \quad s \to (u; c\,t; q).$$

Such a form is mostly used in hydrophysical problems. It shows that to determine the fluxes of momentum, heat and moisture it suffices to have available information on the wind speed, temperature and humidity at some height, on the temperature of the underlying surface, and on the way the coefficient of turbulent exchange varies with altitude. Specific humidity $q(0)$ can be calculated from the water vapor pressure at the temperature of the evaporating surface.

When expressions (4.4) to (4.6) are used in practice, it is essential to determine the ratios between the coefficients of turbulent exchange for different substances. However, owing to the existence of very few direct measurements of the variable components it has not yet been possible to obtain accurate quantitative relationships between the coefficients of momentum, heat and moisture exchange. The similarity of the transfer of different substances and the equality of the exchange coefficients are taken as a first approximation. Such a hypothesis seems natural for passively transferred substances and for conservative substances over a smooth underlying surface. Momentum and heat are not exactly such substances, and their transfer mechanism is different (especially if there is temperature-nonuniform stratification over rough surfaces). But if no reliable relationships exist, the hypothesis of equality of the exchange coefficients has to be used even for such conditions, especially as this assumption makes it possible to use numerous wind-speed profile measurements in the practical determination of the coefficient of heat and moisture exchange.

If as a first approximation $k_\tau = k_t = k_q = k$, expressions (4.5) and (4.6) for the fluxes of heat and moisture are

$$P = c\,\rho C (t_{h_0} - t_0) u_{h_0};$$

$$W = \rho C (q_{h_0} - q_0) u_{h_0}.$$

The drag is then

$$C = \frac{\tau}{\rho u_{h_0}^2} = \frac{1}{u_{h_0}} \left[\int_0^{h_0} \frac{dz}{(k+\nu)} \right]^{-1}. \qquad (4.7)$$

A quantitative description of the main turbulence characteristics and the profiles of the meteorological elements in the temperature-stratified ground layer over the underlying surface with fixed roughness elements is provided by the Monin–Obukhov similarity theory /63, 29/. According to this theory, there exists near the underlying surface a sublayer in which the turbulence is determined solely by dynamic factors, and the effect of the temperature stratification may be neglected. The height of this sublayer of dynamic turbulence is determined by the Monin–Obukhov scale

$$L = -\frac{v_*^3 T}{\varkappa g P / c_p \rho},$$

where $v_* = \sqrt{\frac{\tau}{\rho}}$ is the dynamic velocity, T is the mean absolute temperature, g is the acceleration of gravity, $\varkappa = 0.4$ is the Karman constant.

For altitudes $z \ll L$ conditions over the rough surface approach equilibrium, the wind profile follows the logarithmic law

$$u(z) = \frac{v_*}{\varkappa} \ln \frac{z + z_0}{z_0},$$

and the coefficient of turbulent exchange increases linearly with altitude:

$$k(z) = \varkappa v_* \cdot (z + z_0),$$

where z_0 is the roughness parameter of the underlying surface.

The dynamic velocity and the roughness parameter are quite simply and reliably determined from wind profile measurements. The resistance coefficient, and hence the heat and moisture fluxes, can be easily calculated from known values of these quantities and with the aid of formula (4.7).

The deviation of the temperature stratification in the ground layer from the equilibrium condition causes the wind, temperature and moisture profiles to deviate from the logarithmic function. The stratification conditions can be described quantitatively by the dimensionless ratio $\xi = \frac{z}{L}$ or by the related Richardson number

$$\mathrm{Ri} = \frac{g}{T} \frac{dT/dz}{(du/dz)^2}.$$

The wind, temperature and humidity profiles are in this case expressed in terms of some universal function ξ:

$$u(z) - u(z') = \frac{v_*}{\varkappa} [f_u(\xi) - f_u(\xi')];$$

$$t(z) - t(z') = \frac{\theta_*}{\varkappa} [f_t(\xi) - f_t(\xi')];$$

$$q(z) - q(z') = \frac{q_*}{\varkappa} [f_q(\xi) - f_q(\xi')],$$

where θ_* and q_* are the characteristic temperature and humidity scales:

$$\theta_* = -\frac{P}{c\rho v_*}; \quad q_* = -\frac{W}{\rho l v_*}.$$

Zilitinkevich and Chalikov /30/ processed much experimental material and derived the general form of the universal function under different conditions of stratification:

$$f_u = f_t = f_q = \begin{cases} \ln\xi + a_1\xi & \xi > 0; \\ f|\xi| & \xi_1 \leqslant \xi \leqslant 0; \\ a_2 + a_3\xi^{-1/3} & \xi < \xi_1, \end{cases}$$

where $a_1 = 10.0$, $a_2 = 0.25$, $a_3 = 1.20$, $\xi_1 = -0.07$.

Hence the resistance C, and then the heat and humidity fluxes, can be obtained with a view to deriving the temperature stratification.

Application of the Monin – Obukhov similarity theory to turbulent exchange in the marine surface layer over oceans and seas has been thoroughly investigated by Kitaigorodskii /37/. Specific features distinguishing the marine surface layer over water from the ground layer over dry land are: mobility of the water surface, dynamic interaction between wind and waves, increased atmospheric humidity, substantially complicating the general description of turbulence over lakes and rivers.

In practical calculations great difficulties are posed by the selection of the roughness parameter for the wavy water surface. The values of z_0, calculated from gradient measurements of the wind profile, possess considerable scatter and do not provide a unique dependence on wind speed at a fixed level or on dynamic velocity v_*. If we generalize the available data to the shallow parts of the seas at considerable fetch, we find that z_0 increases slightly with increasing wind speed. As a first approximation the form of this dependence may be taken as linear with values $z_0 = 0.01$ cm at wind speed $u = 2$ m/sec and $z_0 = 0.1$ cm at $u = 14$ m/sec. A similar but more pronounced dependence of the roughness parameter on wind speed is found on inland water bodies /86/. Observations of the sea surface slope and gradient measurements on the high sea suggest an inverse relationship: z_0 decreases with increasing wind speed especially when u is small, and when $u > 3$ m/sec, z_0 is practically constant.

The scatter and contradictions in the relation between the roughness parameter and the wind speed or dynamic velocity can be substantially reduced by allowing for wave mobility, which represents the roughness. If we assume that all the roughness elements move at the same speed u_{ro}, and if we neglect the contribution of low-frequency components of the waves, the roughness parameter can be determined in the form /37/

$$z_0 = 0.120\, h_{av} e^{-\varkappa u_{ro}/v_*}, \quad u_{ro} = \frac{g\tau_{av}}{2\pi},$$

where h_{av} is the mean height and τ_{av} is the mean wave period. It is furthermore shown that the roughness parameter, found by processing individual profile measurements, can be considered as possessing a normal distribution of the random functions of dynamic velocity. The mean value $\bar{z}_0$ of such a statistical population of individual realizations under different conditions can be expressed approximately in the form

$$\bar{z}_0 = 0.035\, v_*^2/g.$$

The interaction of wind and waves leads to the existence of some "sublayer of interaction" within which the reaction of the air to the wave resistance must be taken into account. The total momentum within such a sublayer is the sum of purely turbulent Reynolds stresses, viscous stresses, and the momentum due to the interaction of wave distortions with the mean velocity profile. This latter momentum is the smaller, the greater the distance from the wavy surface, but may generally represent a considerable part of the total momentum flux. At the initial stage of wave development the height of the sublayer is small and the effect of the wave resistance alone cannot be ascertained from the available data; therefore the logarithmic profile of the velocity and the dependence for the roughness parameter remain correct. In the case of swell the thickness of the sublayer of interaction can be commensurable with the height of individual levels at which the wind speed is measured, and deviations from the logarithmic profile are observed due to the effect of the wave resistance /26/. However, there are as yet insufficient experimental data for revealing the quantitative effect of this sublayer on the turbulence characteristics in the marine surface layer.

The effect of high humidity over water bodies on the turbulence characteristics makes itself felt mainly by changes in the conditions of stratification and hydrostatic stability. Quantitative stability criteria (height of sublayer of dynamic turbulence, Richardson number, etc.) are found as a function of the heat and humidity fluxes /28/:

$$\tilde{L} = L\left(1 + \frac{m}{\mathbf{B}_0}\right)^{-1}; \tag{4.8}$$

$$\tilde{\mathbf{Ri}} = \mathbf{Ri}\left(1 + \frac{m}{\mathbf{B}_0}\right), \tag{4.9}$$

where $m = \frac{0.61\, c_p t}{l} \approx 0.07$, $\mathbf{B}_0 = \frac{P}{lW}$ is the Bowen number, and l is the heat of vaporization; L and $\mathbf{Ri}$ are the height of the sublayer of dynamic turbulence and the Richardson number, respectively, and depend solely on the temperature stratification.

Thus, when the Monin–Obukhov similarity theory is applied to the calculation of turbulence characteristics and also of the heat and humidity fluxes in the marine surface layer, the stability criteria must be changed in line with (4.8) or (4.9). Processing of observation data over the sea /37/ shows that the effect of humidity on density stratification can be substantial.

§5. TURBULENT HEAT EXCHANGE IN WATER

The propagation of heat and equalization of temperature in lakes and rivers is effected by advection and turbulent displacement of water masses. These processes are described quantitatively by the equations of turbulent transport which are obtained by averaging the corresponding balance equations of momentum, heat and mass for the instantaneous values of the transported property. Different forms of the equations of turbulent transport may be obtained, depending on the averaging method employed /87, 32/.

Each balance equation for the instantaneous values of the transported property can be expressed in the form

$$\frac{\partial \rho s}{\partial \tau} + \frac{\partial}{\partial x_k} \rho v_k s = \Phi(\rho s), \tag{5.1}$$

where v_k are the flux velocity components, Φ are the sources and sinks of the transported property s per unit mass, and summation is from unity to three for subscripts appearing twice in the same term.

In momentum transfer, s designates the corresponding component of velocity; in heat transfer it denotes the heat content, in the transport of salts the salinity of the water, and in mass transfer $s=1$. The function of the sources and sinks of the transported property includes processes of molecular transfer, viscous dissipation, and specific sources and sinks for the corresponding s.

Consider the instantaneous values of the variable fields in equation (5.1) in the form

$$\rho = \bar{\rho} + \rho', \; s = s + \bar{s}', \; v_k = \bar{v}_k + v_k',$$

where a bar designates averaged values after Reynolds, and a prime designates the fluctuation about the corresponding value. Substitution of these expressions in the balance equations and subsequent averaging yields

$$\bar{\rho}\frac{d\bar{s}}{d\tau} + \frac{d}{d\tau}\overline{\rho' s'} + \overline{\rho' s'}\frac{\partial \bar{v}_k}{\partial x_k} + \overline{\rho' v_k'}\frac{\partial \bar{s}}{\partial x_k} + $$
$$+ \frac{\partial}{\partial x_k}(\bar{\rho}\, \overline{v_\kappa' s'} + \overline{\rho' v_k' s'}) = \bar{\Phi}(\rho s). \tag{5.2}$$

The main difference between these equations and the corresponding equations for an incompressible liquid is that the components with fluctuating density are characteristic of mass transfer. These components are neglected in the usual equations of heat and salt transfer in the sea, and so it is implicitly assumed that transfer of heat and salts compensates mass transfer.

The density of sea water is a function of temperature, salinity S, and pressure. Variations in these quantities cause corresponding variations in density. The usual incompressibility conditions (especially neglecting pressure variations) assumed in hydrodynamics are insufficient for the nonuniformly heated sea water. If we neglect variations in pressure, then

$$\rho' = \frac{\partial \bar{\rho}}{\partial t} t' + \frac{\partial \rho}{\partial \bar{S}} S'. \tag{5.3}$$

It can hardly be expected that under actual conditions the relation $\rho' = 0$ is always maintained, since turbulent variations in temperature and salinity have a random character.

Expression (5.3) is now substituted in (5.2) for heat and salt transfer. If we neglect third-order correlation moments, assume that the mean-square temperature and salinity fluctuations are steady and homogeneous, and further assume that there is no statistical correlation between t' and S', then the corresponding transfer equation becomes

$$\bar{\rho}\frac{d\bar{t}}{d\tau}+\left\{\frac{\partial\bar{\rho}}{d\bar{t}}\overline{v_k't'}+\frac{\partial\bar{\rho}}{\partial S}\overline{v_k'S'}\right\}\frac{\partial t_k}{\partial x_k}+$$

$$+\frac{\partial}{\partial x_k}\bar{\rho}\,v_k't'=\frac{1}{c}\bar{\Phi}_t$$

and, when we replace $c\bar{t}$ by s, the analogous salinity equation is

$$\bar{\rho}\frac{d\bar{S}}{d\tau}+\left\{\frac{\partial\bar{\rho}}{\partial\bar{t}}\overline{v_k't'}+\frac{\partial\bar{\rho}}{\partial\bar{S}}\overline{v_k'S'}\right\}\frac{\partial\bar{S}_k}{\partial x_k}+$$

$$+\frac{\partial}{\partial x_k}\bar{\rho}\,\overline{v_k'S'}=\Phi_s.$$

If a scalar exchange coefficient is taken in the form

$$\overline{v_k't'}=-k_t/\frac{\partial\bar{t}}{\partial z}, \qquad (5.4)$$

we obtain

$$\frac{d\bar{t}}{d\tau}=\frac{\partial}{\partial x_k}k_t\frac{\partial\bar{t}}{\partial x_k}+\frac{2k_t}{\bar{\rho}}\frac{\partial\bar{\rho}}{\partial x_k}\frac{\partial\bar{t}}{\partial x_k}+\frac{1}{c\bar{\rho}}\Phi_t, \qquad (5.5)$$

$$\frac{ds}{d\tau}\quad\frac{\partial}{\partial x_k}k_s\frac{\partial\bar{S}}{\partial x_k}+\frac{2k_s}{\bar{\rho}}\frac{\partial\bar{\rho}}{\partial x_k}\frac{\partial\bar{S}}{\partial x_k}+\frac{1}{\rho}\Phi_s. \qquad (5.6)$$

Alternatively, if we combine the first two terms on the right-hand side

$$\frac{d\bar{t}}{d\tau}=\frac{1}{\bar{\rho}^2}\frac{\partial}{\partial x_k}\left\{\bar{\rho}^2k_t\frac{\partial\bar{t}}{\partial x_k}\right\}+\frac{1}{c\bar{\rho}}\Phi_t, \qquad (5.7)$$

$$\frac{d\bar{s}}{d\tau}=\frac{1}{\bar{\rho}^2}\frac{\partial}{\partial x_k}\left\{\bar{\rho}^2k_s\frac{d\bar{S}}{\partial x_k}\right\}+\frac{1}{\bar{\rho}}\Phi_s. \qquad (5.8)$$

The equations are analogous to (5.5) and (5.6). In the absence of three-dimensional sources of heat or salts they were derived differently by Schmitz /103/.

It is evident that the equations reduce to ordinary equations of salinity or enthalpy transfer only when the density gradient in the water is equal to zero. This limits their applicability to the full description of temperature and salinity distribution in a sea whose density is stratified, especially if there are layers with very pronounced temperature or salinity gradients.

In the general case of a body of water with stratified density the equations of heat and salt transfer must be examined together with the equations of motion and the equation of state. If the velocity field is given, equations (5.5) and (5.6) or (5.7) and (5.8) can be used separately only when the density distribution is determined solely by the inhomogeneity of temperature and pressure (fresh-water) or by the inhomogeneity in the distribution of salinity and pressure. In such cases the density distribution, indispensable for solving the transfer equations, is uniquely determined from the equation of state via the temperature and pressure with salinity constant, or via salinity and pressure with temperature constant.

Because these processes are complicated and insufficiently studied, we confine ourselves mainly to an examination of thermal and ice phenomena in freshwater bodies where the velocity field of the flow is known and the actual conditions are correspondingly schematized. Analysis of observations indicates that in the open parts of water bodies the vertical gradients of temperature and density are considerably greater than the horizontal gradients. As for the marine surface layer, we may assume in a first approximation that the statistical characteristics and mean values change only vertically if there are no permanent currents. If currents exist, heat advection must also be taken into account. As a result of this schematization we obtain a theoretical model for describing turbulent heat transfer: vertical heat transfer is effected by exchange, horizontal heat transfer by advection of the water masses. If under these conditions the origin of coordinates is taken at the surface of the water body, the $0z$ axis is directed vertically downward and the axis $0x$ points in the direction of the center current, then the temperature field in the water is described by the equation

$$\frac{\partial \bar{t}}{\partial \tau} + \bar{v}\frac{\partial \bar{t}}{\partial x} = \frac{1}{\rho^2}\frac{\partial}{\partial z}\left(\bar{\rho}^2 k \frac{\partial \bar{t}}{\partial z}\right) + \frac{1}{c\bar{\rho}}\Phi_t. \tag{5.9}$$

If the processes of molecular transfer, dissipation of mechanical energy, and chemical and biological phenomena are neglected, the form of the function is determined by the absorption of radiant energy in the water. In that case expression (2.6) can be used to derive

$$\Phi_t = -\frac{\partial Q(z,\tau)}{\partial z} = Q_0(\tau) \sum_{m=1}^{\nu} I_m \beta_m e^{-\beta_m z}. \quad (5.10)$$

To solve (5.9) uniquely with the aid of (5.10), it is necessary to stipulate corresponding boundary and initial conditions, equation of state $\bar{\rho}=\bar{\rho}(t)$, and the dependence of k on the factors determining it.

The coefficients of turbulent heat exchange can be determined from experimental data in two ways: one is the "direct" method based on the exchange coefficient taken in the form (5.4), the other is the "indirect" method using the transfer equations or their particular solutions. Initial data for the direct method comprise the simultaneous recording of the variable components and the mean gradient of the transferred property. Apparatus and methods for such measurements have been successfully developed in recent years, but as yet there exist only isolated measurement data and turbulent exchange coefficients calculated on their basis /8, 83, 65/.

When indirect methods are used, information is needed only on the mean characteristics of the transferred property. The transfer coefficients, calculated by these methods, express the simultaneous action of the thermal and dynamic conditions in the water body, and therefore their scatter is greater. The accuracy of calculations by different methods is determined by agreement of the initial data with the accepted schematization of the problem on which some method or other is based. To solve the main problem, i. e., to establish a relationship between the turbulent exchange coefficients and the hydrometeorological factors, it is necessary to simultaneously measure all the basic elements of the thermohydrodynamic regime of the water body and the marine surface layer. No such full-scale investigations have been conducted yet.

Of the many methods of calculating turbulent exchange coefficients we shall first examine the method of temperature waves. Its advantage is that it allows one to determine the validity of the initial observation data and the time-averaging interval pertaining to the values that were obtained for the turbulent exchange coefficients. The first calculation methods of this group were proposed by Schmidt and Fjeldstad /101/ on the basis of the problem of temperature wave propagation in a uniformly dense deep sea in the absence of three-dimensional heat sources. Anisimova and Pivovarov /2/ generalized Fjeldstad's method and allowed for the latter factor. They expressed the water temperature variation at any depth and the radiant energy flux entering the sea in the form of Fourier series (the bar above mean values is omitted):

$$t(z, \tau) = \sum_{n=1}^{\infty} A_n' \cos n\omega\tau + A_n'' \sin n\omega\tau =$$

$$= \sum_{n-1}^{\infty} A_n \cos (n\omega\tau - \varphi_n),$$

$$\frac{Q_0(\tau)}{c\rho} = \sum_{n=1}^{\infty} B_n' \cos n\omega\tau + B_n'' \sin n\omega\tau.$$

Using equation (5.9) and (5.10), with $\bar{v} = 0$ and $\bar{\rho} =$ const, they derived the following expression for the turbulent exchange coefficient:

$$k(z_1) = \frac{\left(A_n^2 \frac{d\varphi_n}{dz}\right) z = z_2}{\left(A_n^2 \frac{d\varphi_n}{dz}\right) z = z_1} k(z_2) + \frac{\int\limits_{z_1}^{z_2} (n\omega A_n^2 - s_{n,m})\, dz}{\left(A_n^2 \frac{d\varphi_n}{dz}\right) z = z_1}, \tag{5.11}$$

where

$$s_{n,m} = (A_n'' B_n' - A_n' B_n'') \sum_{m=1}^{\nu} I_m \beta_m e^{-\beta_m z}.$$

If the lower boundary is selected as $z_2 = h$ and $A_n(h) = 0$ and $s_{n,m} = 0$ (no three-dimensional heat sources), expression (5.11) reduces to Fjeldstad's formula

$$k(z) = \frac{n\omega}{A_n^2 \frac{d\varphi_n}{dz}} \int\limits_z^h A_n^2(z)\, dz. \tag{5.12}$$

Formulas (5.11) and (5.12) do not yield values of the coefficient of turbulent exchange when $z = h$ or $z = z_2$. To exclude this indeterminacy, (5.11) may be applied to two harmonics of the temperature wave or to thin layers, taking $k =$ const within such a layer; alternatively the calculation can be conducted beginning with depths $z > h$ at which practically $A_n(h) = 0$. The corresponding expressions can be obtained easily from (5.11).

More general than the methods of temperature waves are balance methods of calculating turbulent exchange coefficients based directly on the integration of equation (5.9) (taking (5.10) into account) from the surface to some depth z which, with $\bar{v}=0$ and $\bar{\rho}=$const, yields

$$\int_0^z \frac{\partial t}{\partial \tau}\,dz = \left(k\frac{\partial t}{\partial z}\right)_z - \left(k\frac{\partial t}{\partial z}\right)_0 + \\ + \frac{Q_0(\tau)}{c\rho}\sum_{m=1}^{\nu} I_m\beta_m \int_0^z e^{-\beta_m z}\,dz.$$

The heat balance equation allowing for the main components of (1.3) gives

$$k(z,\tau) = \frac{-R \pm P \pm lW + Q_0 \sum_{m=1}^{\nu} I_m\beta_m \int_0^z e^{-\beta_m z}\,dz - c\rho \int_0^z \frac{\partial t}{\partial \tau}\,dz}{c\rho\,(\partial t/\partial z)_{z=0}}$$

When balance methods are used, many initial data are needed and the calculation accuracy is determined from them not only by the agreement of the initial heat transfer equation in the water with actual conditions, but also by the accuracy of describing and measuring the components of heat exchange with the atmosphere at the water – air interface. All this considerably limits calculation of the coefficients of turbulent heat exchange on a mass scale by balance methods.

If no data exist on the components of heat exchange with the atmosphere, balance methods can be used to find changes in $k(z,\tau)$ by integrating the main equation from some depth z_1 to z_2:

$$k(z_1,\tau) = \frac{\left[k\left(\frac{\partial t}{\partial z}\right)\right]_{z_2} + \frac{Q_0}{c\rho}\sum_{m=1}^{\nu} I_m\beta_m \int_0^z e^{-\beta_m z} - \int_{z_1}^{z_2} \frac{\partial t}{\partial \tau}\,dz}{(\partial t/\partial z)_1}.$$

Quantity $k_2(z,\tau)$ must be determined by some other independent method.

A similar analysis of vertical turbulent mixing in the surface layer of the sea, in the presence of wind-driven waves, is given by Kitaigorodskii /37/, who shows that the change in the coefficient of turbulent viscosity is described by a curve with maximum at some depth below the surface of the sea whose position and magnitude depend on the stage of wave development. However, calculations of this coefficient have so far not been compared with data of direct measurements or calculations by indirect methods, because the required measurements are unavailable.

The effect of density stratification on vertical turbulent exchange is taken into account qualitatively by the Richardson number **Ri** or the stability E_0 of the water masses. For the sea

$$\mathbf{Ri} = E_0 / \left(\frac{\partial u}{\partial z}\right)^2,$$

$$E_0 = \frac{g}{\rho}\left\{\frac{\partial \rho}{\partial t}\left[\frac{dt}{dz} - \left(\frac{dt}{dz}\right)_A\right] + \frac{\partial \rho}{\partial S}\frac{dS}{dz}\right\},$$

where $\left(\frac{dt}{dz}\right)_A$ is the adiabatic temperature gradient. In shallow freshwater lakes the Richardson number or the stability is determined by the velocity and temperature gradients alone.

When the effect of density stratification is taken into account, the turbulent exchange coefficient is

$$k_c = k_0 (1 - \eta \mathbf{Ri}),$$

$$k_c = k_0 (1 + b \mathbf{Ri})^{-1}.$$

These expressions yield similar results when the empirical parameter $b = 2\eta$ and when $0 \leqslant \mathbf{Ri} \leqslant 1/\eta$.

Consider some data obtained from calculations of the coefficient of turbulent heat exchange by various indirect methods /2, 19/. Figure 6 shows that if the volume absorption of solar radiation is neglected, it leads to a qualitatively different vertical course of the turbulent exchange coefficient in water layers near the surface. The physical cause of such deviations becomes clear if we remember that the water temperature near the surface is not only the result of turbulent transfer, but also of direct radiative heating owing to the absorption of radiant energy. Neglect of this factor in the basic equation of heat propagation naturally results in higher coefficients of turbulent exchange. A decrease in the coefficient of turbulent exchange nearer the water surface, obtained in calculations by indirect methods with allowance for volume absorption of radiant energy, is physically more plausible than its increase.

Figure 7 shows the daily course of the turbulent exchange coefficient at different depths, calculated from measurement data for clear sky and in the absence of waves. Maximum values of k occur at night, minimum values in daytime; this corresponds to the diurnal course of stability. The amplitude of the oscillations of k decreases with increasing depth, and at a depth of more than 5 m there is practically no longer any diurnal course.

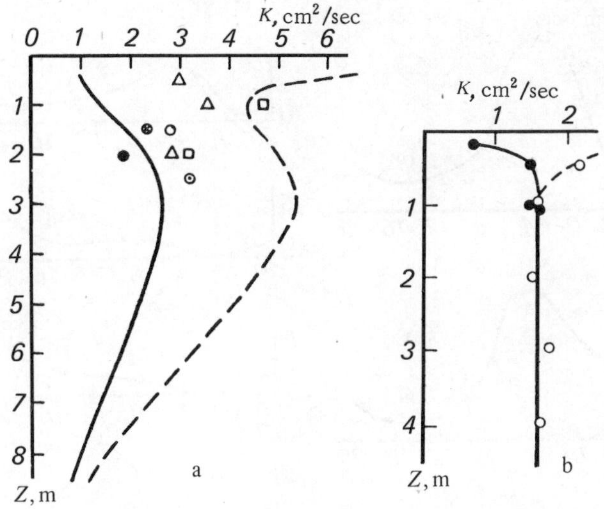

FIGURE 6. Depth variation in coefficient of turbulent heat exchange:

a — Black Sea; b — Uchinskoe Reservoir.
——— taking into account, ---- — not taking into account, volume absorption of radiant energy by the balance method; dots correspond to the method of temperature waves.

Many calculations of mean daily and mean annual values of *k* as a function of depth have been conducted /90, 35, 8, 17, 43, etc./. These calculations yield qualitatively the same results for different seas: minimum turbulent exchange coefficients correspond to layers of maximum stability. For inland water bodies such calculations of *k* have so far been carried out only sporadically.

§6. HEAT EXCHANGE WITH THE BOTTOM IN SHALLOW LAKES AND RIVERS

Thermal conditions in shallow lakes and rivers, especially before and during the ice period, are to a large extent dependent on heat exchange between the water masses and the bottom. The magnitude of this heat exchange is mainly determined by two processes: heat transfer in the bottom soil via heat conduction, and heat transfer by groundwater. In regard to groundwater this process has not yet been adequately solved. However, for lakes and storage lakes that are relatively large in area and of about the same depth throughout it may be assumed that heat transfer by groundwater, except in parts close to the shores, is minimal and that heat propagation in the bottom soil is effected mainly through conduction.

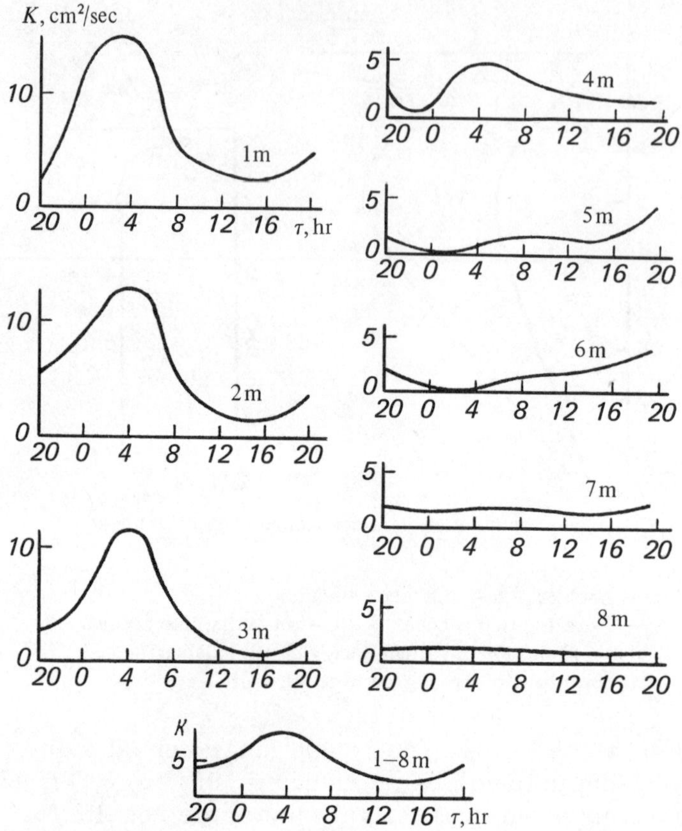

FIGURE 7. Diurnal course of the coefficient of turbulent heat exchange at different depths in the Black Sea /20/.

Direct measurements of the temperature gradients and thermal characteristics in the bottom soil would require special and laborious investigations, which so far have not been attempted. Direct measurements of heat fluxes in the bottom soil by thermometers /50/ are sporadic /83/. Heat exchange between the bottom and the water masses must therefore be determined theoretically.

Existing methods of calculating the temperature field in the bottom soil of lakes and its heat exchange with the water masses can be divided into two groups. One group contains methods that regard as known the main heat balance components on the water surface as a function of time; the other group contains methods that use as initial data the temperature variation of the bottom layers of the water identifiable with the temperature variation of the surface of the bottom soil.

In the first case the temperature field in the bottom soil is given by the ordinary solution of the heat exchange equations in the water and in the bottom subject to heat balance on the water surface. In that case the theoretical relationships are cumbersome and unreliable, owing to their complicated dependence on many factors of turbulent heat exchange in the water and the heat balance components on the surface.

The second method is mathematically simple and yields more reliable results, because only one parameter characterizing the thermal properties of the bottom and the measured water temperature near the bottom are contained in the computation relationships. Temperature measurements near the bottom, however, limit this method considerably in calculations of heat exchange with the bottom in newly planned storage lakes, or in the ice period when the water temperature near the bottom is itself an unknown function. But as a rule, in all practical methods of computing heat exchange of the water with the bottom, the temperature of the surface of the bottom soil is regarded as known, and the temperature field below the bottom is determined from the solution of the one-dimensional heat propagation equation

$$\frac{\partial t_b}{\partial \tau} = k_b \frac{\partial^2 t_b}{\partial z^2} \tag{6.1}$$

with boundary conditions

$$\begin{aligned} z = 0 \quad & t = \theta_b(\tau), \\ z \to \infty \quad & t = \text{const}, \end{aligned} \tag{6.2}$$

where k_b is the coefficient of molecular heat conductivity of the bottom. The origin of coordinates is situated on the surface of the bottom soil, and the Oz axis is directed vertically downward from the bottom into the soil.

The difference in the methods of calculating the heat exchange of water with the bottom, based on the solutions of equations (6.1) with conditions (6.2), is mainly due to the nature of the approximations of the temperature variation of the surface of the bottom soil $\theta_b(\tau)$ and the selected initial distribution.

The method of temperature waves with a period of one year expresses approximation $\theta_b(\tau)$ by a Fourier series, after which the periodic solution of (6.1) with conditions (6.2) is determined /56, 40/. This method yields very good results for the summer period or for lakes that do not freeze, when $\theta_b(\tau)$ is indeed close to a part of or the entire harmonic curve. However, when the full annual course of the heat exchange with the bottom is to be calculated for freezing lakes and rivers, approximation $\theta_b(\tau)$ requires a large number of terms of the Fourier series, which makes the calculation extremely cumbersome.

The method proposed by Rossinskii /58/ averages the actual course of θ_b within some time interval, and then the initial temperature distribution below the bottom is taken as zero, but this initial instant is transferred to "an indeterminately distant past." In practice this is achieved by including in the calculation several years in succession. The temperature of the near-bottom water layers is averaged for the calculated year by months, for the preceding year for the summer and the winter periods, and for the entire time before that within one degree of the mean long-term temperature. The heat flux on the surface of the bottom soil, obtained by solving equation (6.1), is also represented in the form of a stepped curve along which a smooth curve is then drawn. Such an approximation corresponds more to the course of the water temperature in winter under the ice cover, but when applied to the summer period it gives rise to substantial errors.

It is not difficult to eliminate these shortcomings and derive simple and reliable relationships for calculating the temperature field below the bottom on the basis of the following considerations /69/. The temperature waves of the annual period propagating from the surface of the bottom soil penetrate only to a certain depth, beneath which the temperature remains practically constant and equal to the mean long-term temperature θ_b of the near-bottom water layers. When the ice cover disintegrates and melts, the deviations in the temperature distribution from its long-term mean in the layer of the propagation of temperature fluctuations are minimal, and their effect on the formation of the temperature field below the bottom decreases rapidly with the onset of summer heating of the water. Just as the time of ice breakup on the water surface is chosen as initial time, so the initial temperature distribution in the bottom soil may be assumed to be the mean long-term temperature θ_b of the near-bottom layers of the water:

$$\tau = 0, \quad t_b(0, z) = \bar{\theta}_b = \text{const.} \tag{6.3}$$

The solution to equation (6.1) with conditions (6.2) and (6.3) is

$$t_b(z, \tau) = \frac{2\bar{\theta}_b}{\sqrt{\pi}} \int\limits_0^{z/2\sqrt{k_b\tau}} e^{-\xi^2} d\xi + \frac{z}{2\sqrt{\pi k_b}} \int\limits_0^{\tau} \frac{\theta_b(\eta)\, e^{-\frac{z^2}{4k_b(\tau-\eta)}}}{\sqrt{(\tau-\eta)^3}} d\eta. \tag{6.4}$$

Since in practice only discrete values of the bottom temperature of the water θ_m are known at times τ_m, the approximation of $\theta_b(\tau)$

by a piecewise linear function is expedient. The calculation method can be considerably simplified and standardized by stipulating θ_m with equal time intervals s, where

$$\theta_b(\tau) = \theta_m + (\theta_{m+1} - \theta_m)\frac{\tau - ms}{s}, \quad ms \leqslant \tau \leqslant (m+1)s.$$

If we substitute this expression in (6.4) and integrate, we obtain

$$t_b(z, Ps) = \bar{\theta}_b \operatorname{erf}\left(\frac{z}{2\sqrt{k_b Ps}}\right) + 4\sum_{m=0}^{P} \theta_m \cdot \Phi_{m,P}, \tag{6.5}$$

where

$$\Phi_0 = (P-1)\, i^2 \operatorname{erfc}\left(\frac{x}{\sqrt{P-1}}\right) - Pi^2 \operatorname{erfc}\frac{x}{\sqrt{P}} + $$

$$+ 0.25 \operatorname{erfc}\frac{x}{\sqrt{P}},$$

$$\Phi_P = i^2 \operatorname{erfc} x,$$

$$\Phi_{m,P} = (P-m+1)\, i^2 \operatorname{erfc}\frac{x}{\sqrt{P-m+1}} +$$

$$+ (P-m-1)\, i^2 \operatorname{erfc}\frac{x}{\sqrt{P-m-1}} -$$

$$-2(P-m)\, i^2 \operatorname{erfc}\frac{x}{\sqrt{P-m}};$$

$$x = \frac{z}{2\sqrt{k_1 s}}; \quad \operatorname{erfc} x = 1 - \operatorname{erf} x;$$

$$\operatorname{erfc} x = \frac{2}{\sqrt{\pi}}\int_0^x e^{-\xi^2} d\xi;$$

$$i^2 \operatorname{erfc} x = \frac{1}{4}\left[(1+2x^2)\operatorname{erfc} x - \frac{2}{\sqrt{\pi}}\, x e^{-x^2}\right].$$

Expression (6.5) gives in explicit form the temperature in the ground at any depth for $\tau = Ps$. Since this expression contains detailed tabulated functions of the error integral erf x and exponential functions, the calculation does not present any fundamental difficulties.

The theoretical expression for the heat exchange with water is obtained from (6.5) by differentiating with respect to z and multiplying the result by the coefficient of heat conductivity λ_b of the bottom. Hence the heat flux from the bottom of the water body is $Q_b = \lambda_b \frac{\partial t_b}{\partial z}$, or

$$Q_b = \frac{2\sqrt{\lambda_b c_b \rho_b}}{\sqrt{\pi s}} \left[\frac{\bar{\theta}_b - \theta_0}{2\sqrt{P}} + \sum_{m=0}^{P} \theta_m \Psi_{m,P} \right], \tag{6.6}$$

where

$$\Psi_{m,P} = \begin{cases} \sqrt{P} - \sqrt{P-1} & (m = 0), \\ 2\sqrt{P-m} - \sqrt{P-m-1} - \sqrt{P-m+1} & (1 \leqslant m \leqslant P-1). \\ -1 & (m = P). \end{cases}$$

TABLE 6. Function $\Psi_{m,P} \cdot 10^3$ for calculating heat exchange with the bottom*

P	m								
	0	1	2	3	4	5	6	7	8
2	414	586							
3	318	96.4	586						
4	268	49.9	96.4	586					
5	236	31.9	49.9	96.4	586				
6	213	22.6	31.9	49.9	96.4	586			
7	196	17.2	22.6	31.9	49.9	96.4	586		
8	183	13.6	17.2	22.6	31.9	49.9	96.4	586	
9	172	11.1	13.6	17.2	22.6	31.9	49.9	96.4	586
10	162	9.29	11.1	13.6	17.2	22.6	31.9	49.9	96.4
11	154	7.94	9.29	11.1	13.6	17.2	22.6	31.9	49.9
12	148	6.87	7.94	9.29	11.1	13.6	17.2	22.6	31.9
13	141	6.03	6.87	7.94	9.29	11.1	13.6	17.2	22.6
14	136	5.34	6.03	6.87	7.94	9.29	11.1	13.6	17.2
15	131	4.78	5.34	6.03	6.87	7.94	9.29	11.1	13.6
16	127	4.31	4.78	5.34	6.03	6.87	7.94	9.29	11.1
17	123	3.91	4.31	4.78	5.34	6.03	6.87	7.94	9.29
18	119	3.57	3.91	4.31	4.78	5.34	6.03	6.87	7.94
19	116	3.28	3.57	3.91	4.31	4.78	5.34	6.03	6.87
20	113	3.02	3.28	3.57	3.91	4.31	4.78	5.34	6.03
21	110	2.80	3.02	3.28	3.57	3.91	4.31	4.78	5.34
22	108	2.60	2.80	3.02	3.28	3.57	3.91	4.31	4.78
23	105	2.42	2.60	2.80	3.02	3.28	3.57	3.91	4.31
24	103	2.27	2.42	2.60	2.80	3.02	3.28	3.57	3.91
25	101	2.13	2.27	2.42	2.60	2.80	3.02	3.28	3.57
26	99.0	2.00	2.13	2.27	2.42	2.60	2.80	3.02	3.28
27	97.1	1.89	2.00	2.13	2.27	2.42	2.60	2.80	3.02
28	95.4	1.78	1.89	2.00	2.13	2.27	2.42	2.60	2.80
29	94.4	1.69	1.78	1.89	2.00	2.13	2.27	2.42	2.60
30	93.7	1.60	1.69	1.78	1.89	2.00	2.13	2.27	2.42
31	93.0	1.52	1.60	1.69	1.78	1.89	2.00	2.13	2.27
32	90.6	1.45	1.52	1.60	1.69	1.78	1.89	2.00	2.13
33	89.0	1.38	1.45	1.52	1.60	1.69	1.78	1.89	2.00
34	87.8	1.32	1.38	1.45	1.52	1.60	1.69	1.78	1.89
35	86.4	1.26	1.32	1.38	1.45	1.52	1.60	1.69	1.78

* Extension of the table for $m = 9, 10 \ldots 34$ can be carried out automatically. The numbers of the m-th column are obtained by transposing the numbers of the $(m-1)$-th column to the line below. The part of the table given here illustrates its compilation.

Since function $\Psi_{m,p}$ does not contain any characteristics of the bottom, the tabulated values of these functions, once compiled, are universal (Table 6). This makes it possible to easily calculate the annual course of the heat exchange of the water with the bottom, the interval of linear approximation of the course of bottom temperatures equaling 10 days.

To simplify calculations of the temperature distribution below the bottom for any time, functions $\Phi_{m,p}$ in (6.5) can also be easily tabulated for different fixed values of z and coefficients of thermal conductivity k_b of the bottom. The construction of such tables is simple.

Figure 8 contains a comparison of the temperature distribution below the bottom, calculated by (6.5) at the instant of freezing in two lakes, with the calculation by Korytnikova /56/ by the method of thermal waves with a Fourier-series approximation of $\theta_b(\tau)$ containing 12 terms. The discrepancy in the calculated curves for both cases does not exceed 5% at any depth, which is within the accuracy of the assigned $\theta_b(\tau)$ according to the approximating curve with linear approximation interval equal to 1 month.

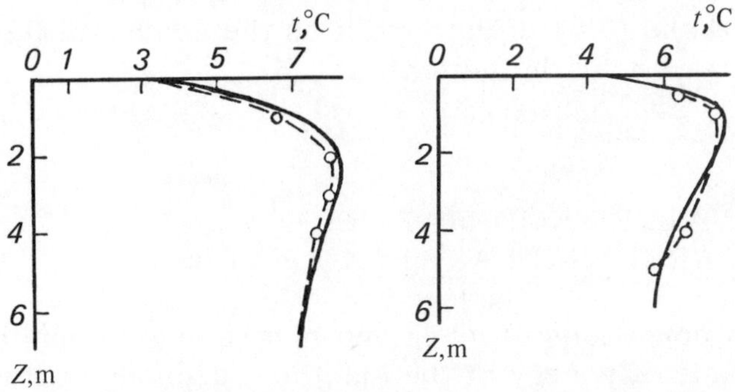

FIGURE 8. Temperature distribution below the bottom at the instant of freezing:

a — Lake Beloe; b — Lake Sardonakh; ——— by formula (6.5); ---- — by the method of thermal waves.

Figure 9 contains a comparison of the annual course of the heat exchange of the bottom with the water masses for the storage lake, calculated by (6.6) and by Rossinskii's method /58/. There is good agreement between the calculated heat exchange in the course of the entire year. However, calculations by (6.6) yield a continuous course of Q_b and require no additional smoothing, which is not the case with Rossinskii's method.

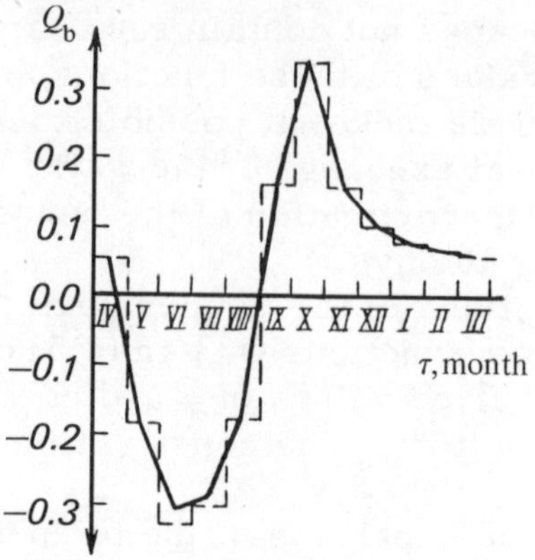

FIGURE 9. Time variation of thermal flux from the bottom of Kama Reservoir: ——— by formula (6.6); ---- — by Rossinskii's method.

Thus the temperature field below the bottom and its heat exchange with the water masses can be calculated quite simply and reliably by (6.5) and (6.6), if data exist on the course of the water temperature at and near the bottom.

§7. ANNUAL WATER TEMPERATURE VARIATION IN FREEZING LAKES AND RIVERS

The thermal conditions of lakes and rivers are determined by the absorption of radiant energy of the sun, heat exchange with the atmosphere and the bottom, and heat transfer in the water by turbulent mixing and advection. The interaction of these factors produces a temperature field which is inhomogeneous in space and unsteady in time. We can pinpoint the most important factors by the hydrological conditions of the water body or the time of year, and by somewhat schematizing the actual conditions we can describe quantitatively the formation of the temperature field.

Two periods are usually distinguished during the annual changes of thermal conditions in freezing lakes and rivers: the summer period, when the water surface is free of ice, and the ice period, beginning when a continuous ice cover forms on the surface and ending with the breakup of the ice cover (this division cannot encompass transient periods of freezing and debacle in which the existence of surface ice or frazil is characteristic).

This subdivision is based on allowance for special features in the formation of thermal conditions in lakes and rivers during these periods. The formation of a continuous ice cover, and later of a snow cover on the surface of the water, greatly changes the conditions of heat exchange with the atmosphere: the total heat exchange of the open water surface with the marine surface layer, which predominates in summer, is replaced by the heat flux through the ice and snow layers. On the lower face of the ice cover the process of ice formation stabilizes the temperature, which equals that of freezing water. The dynamic effect of the atmosphere is almost completely eliminated, and thermal effects find expression mainly by changes in the thickness of the ice and snow cover. These features (cf. Chapter III) make it possible to forecast the temperature field in the water under the ice cover during the entire ice period, using only information on the initial temperature distribution in the water and in the bottom soil at the time of freezing, the characteristics of turbulent heat exchange in the water, and the thermal characteristics of the bottom.

Water temperature measurements bring to light substantial differences in the nature of summer and winter processes /58/. After the ice cover has disintegrated in spring, the water temperature rises, attains a maximum, and then drops again until ice forms. Naturally, the rates of heating and cooling as well as the absolute value of the maximum summer temperature differ, depending on the hydrometeorological conditions of the lake or river, but the general variation in water temperature during the summer period in different water bodies is qualitatively the same. In the ice period the course of the water temperature seems anomalous compared with the summer period, and varies depending on the hydrological properties of the lake or river in question.

The common character of the course is encountered only at the initial time: after a continuous ice cover has formed, the water temperature under the ice rises. In deep or weakly turbulent lakes the rise in water temperature continues all through the winter, gradually slowing down. In shallow or strongly turbulent lakes the water becomes warmer after freezing only to some instant, after which the water temperature begins to drop. In such water bodies the annual course of water temperature is characterized by two maxima: one in summer and one in winter.

In the summer period, after breakup of the ice and establishment of the spring homothermy, gradual warming begins and a thin surface layer of warm water forms. The existence of such a thermally stable layer leads to a reduction in the intensity and depth of turbulent mixing in the absence of wind and currents. The upper heated layer is divided from the underlying layers by a clear drop in temperature (thermocline). The formation of the thermocline is a characteristic feature of the vertical water temperature distribution in summer in deep lakes or lakes with low runoff.

When the water is heated further, the temperature gradually rises and the heated layer increases in thickness, mainly owing to the mechanical action of the wind. When fall cooling begins, the intensity of mixing in the upper layer and its thickness begin to increase considerably faster as a result of the combined action of wind and thermal convection, which act in the same direction until the temperature is attained at which the density is greatest. The temperature gradient in the thermocline gradually decreases, and when the water is relatively shallow the mixing during fall cooling extends all the way down to the bottom; in deep lakes an inverse temperature stratification is established. In shallow and large open lakes the thermocline is encountered in periods of calm weather, but it is quickly destroyed by wind-driven waves, and the vertical temperature distribution is much more even during the entire summer period.

Finally, consider the main features of water temperature formation under the ice cover. Observations in shallow water show that at the beginning of freezing the vertical temperature distribution is fairly uniform, and its absolute value is close to zero. Quite a different picture is presented by the bottom soil: owing to the low thermal conductivity of the soils constituting the bottom, the spring and summer heat reserves cannot be expended during fall cooling, and they are partly retained. Heat exchange with the bottom becomes the main external source for heating the water after freezing.

The rate at which heat is transmitted from the bottom to the underside of the ice cover is determined by the intensity of turbulent heat exchange in the water. In lakes with intensive turbulent exchange the heat reserves of the bottom are transmitted much more rapidly to the water and the underside of the ice cover. After they have been expended the water temperature gradually begins to drop as a result of continued cooling of the surface layers at the water – ice interface. A shallower water body has the same effect. This in particular determines the winter water-temperature maximum under the ice cover in shallow or very turbulent lakes. If the turbulent exchange is not very intensive, the thermal reserves of the bottom are expended more slowly, and the heat emission of the bottom continues throughout the ice period and causes the water temperature to rise continuously.

The fundamental laws governing the course of water temperature in winter, observed in shallow water bodies, remain qualitatively correct also for the surface-layer water temperature in deep lakes. The difference is that the depth of this surface layer is not constant but varies as a function of hydrometeorological factors. In deep lakes the role of the bottom is played by deep water underneath the surface layer in the form of a "liquid bottom."

Chapter II

SUMMER HEATING AND FALL COOLING

§8. STATE OF INVESTIGATIONS AND STATEMENT OF PROBLEM

The study of methods of calculating the temperature field in freezing lakes and rivers in the ice-free period is of great importance in solving a number of economic questions (design and operation of hydraulic and aquicultural structures, determination of navigation periods, etc.). The mathematical statement of water temperature computation in this period is sufficiently determinate, and yields the required initial data for describing the temperature and ice conditions during freezing and in the ice period.

The vertical profile of the water temperature and its time variation in the ice-free period were briefly examined in §7. Only a few direct measurements of the space and time distribution of temperature exist at present. The chief shortcoming of the available data is the lack of synchronized observations of the main actinometric and hydrometeorological elements for calculating the heat balance components. If observations in the coastal zone (conducted by hydrometeorological stations) are not complemented by additional investigations, they cannot be used to compute the elements of the thermal regime in an exposed region or in a water body as a whole. Although we cannot claim to have complete information, we may claim that the most complete observation data of the temperature regime and their generalization pertain to the Rybinsk Reservoir /81/, the storage lakes of the Moscow—Volga system /58/, Lake Baikal /80/, Lake Sevan /86, 23/, and others.

These data show that in the exposed parts of lakes, when the depth is relatively uniform and there are no stable currents, the horizontal temperature distribution is fairly close to uniform. Considerable horizontal temperature gradients may occur in regions with abrupt differences in hydrological and morphometric features. On this assumption, we can quantitatively examine the temperature field in the open part of a lake with approximately equal hydrological parameters and regard it in a first approximation as horizontally homogeneous, changing only with depth and with time. Such an approximation is acceptable in most theoretical studies.

Among practical methods of calculating water temperature in the ice-free period the most widely used method is to establish empirical relations between the water temperature and the chief meteorological factors, especially air temperature. This method disregards the physical nature of processes in the formation of water temperature, and the application of pertinent expressions established on the basis of statistical processing of observation data for some lake and some time of the year, but is limited to those conditions for which the relations were derived.

Studies of the thermal conditions of rivers and lakes showed that the heat balance approach is more efficient. This treatment is based on the application of the integral form of heat balance equation (1.1) pertaining to the conditions existing in the actual lake or river. This method has often been applied when computing the heat balance of seas, lakes, storage lakes, and rivers /82, 77, 92, etc./.

Timofeev /86/ employed the equations of turbulent heat and moisture transfer in the marine surface layer and the equation of turbulent heat transfer in the water. He greatly developed the heat balance method of calculating the surface temperature of water bodies. Introducing an additional hypothesis concerning the relation between the vertically averaged water temperature and the surface temperature, Timofeev succeeded in deriving a simple analytical expression for the surface temperature of a water body as a function of the main components of heat exchange with the atmosphere, the volume absorption of the sun's radiant energy, and the depth of the water body. He studied the resulting solution and emphasized the importance of the thickness of the layer of active heat exchange in the water, which depends on all the hydro-meteorological features of the water body. Water bodies are divided into the following two groups from the standpoint of the relation between the depth of the water body and the thickness of the layer of active heat exchange, within which the vertically averaged and the surface temperatures are closely related.

1. Shallow, very turbulent water bodies with vertically, fairly well distributed temperature, where the layer of active heat exchange extends right down to the bottom. This group comprises most 10 – 15-m-deep open water bodies in the steppes.

2. Deep water bodies in which the layer of active heat exchange is separated from the underlying water by a thermocline. The thickness of the layer of active heat exchange in such water bodies may fluctuate considerably with time.

Timofeev's calculations showed that the depth of a water body has a different effect on surface temperature variations during periods of heating and cooling. In shallow water bodies there is in the former case an inverse correlation, while in the latter case a direct correlation exists in water bodies up to 50 m deep. If the water body is more than 1 km in size, the horizontal dimensions are of little account.

There are very few investigations concerned with the methods of calculating the vertical distribution and time variation of the water temperature. Fall cooling of seas was investigated by Kolesnikov /40/, Lineikin /60/, Kagan /36/ and Zhukov /27/, and storage lakes by Kolesnikov and Pivovarov /45, 49/, Pekhovich /66/ and Rossinskii /104/. A common feature in the analytical approach to these investigations is the application of the one-dimensional equation of turbulent heat transfer in water with an assigned variation in the coefficient of turbulent transfer and corresponding initial and boundary conditions. We retain the same statement of the problem, because it reflects fairly well the actual conditions governing the formation of water temperature in the exposed parts of water bodies. If there are stable currents, advective heat transfer may be regarded as corresponding to the components in the equation of turbulent transfer.

The initial data are taken as the known main actinometric and meteorological elements (which vary with time) at some level in the marine surface layer; the elements comprise the flux of total solar radiation, effective radiation, atmospheric temperature and humidity, wind speed. We also regard as known the albedo of the water, the distribution and type of cloudiness, and the turbulent exchange features in the air and in the water. The heat and moisture fluxes in the marine surface layer are quasi-steady. Hence the stipulation of the main actinometric and meteorological elements at one level enables them to be expressed (in line with the methods of Chapter I) in terms of the main components of heat exchange with the atmosphere. In this way we can determine the effect of the thermal and dynamic regimes in the marine surface layer on the formation of the water temperature. This effect is described quantitatively by the heat balance equation in the form of (1.2) or (1.3), taking into account the corresponding analytical expressions for the main components of these equations.

Such a statement of the problem is usually accepted in hydrophysical investigations, and is only approximate because the stipulated initial data depend to some extent on the thermal conditions of the water body. The greatest difficulty is encountered in stipulating the quantitative characteristics of turbulence in the marine surface layer and in the water. However, the system of turbulent transfer equations for nonsteady processes has not yet been closed in a way suitable for practical application. We must therefore reconcile ourselves to this limitation. But in view of the given turbulence characteristics and the meteorological conditions in the marine surface layer the given statement of the problem is sufficiently general; it yields quantitative results, and permits one to estimate the limit of its applicability.

§9. THE EFFECT OF VOLUME ABSORPTION OF RADIANT ENERGY

It was noted in §1 and §2 that thc absorption of radiant energy in water depends on its transparency. In water with low transparency the flux of radiant energy is almost completely absorbed in the thin surface layer of the water, only a few centimeters thick. In water with high transparency the radiant energy propagates to a considerable depth, and its absorption creates vertically distributed sources of heat. Accordingly, there are at present two versions of the statement of the problem of water-temperature formation in the surface layer of water bodies.

One version allows for volume absorption of the sun's radiant energy. This describes more correctly the physical process of water-temperature formation, but leads to relations that are very complicated for practical calculations and require a large amount of initial data. The second version assumes that the entire flux of radiant energy entering the water is completely absorbed at the water surface, and it is taken into account as the corresponding component only in the boundary conditions. This approach yields simpler theoretical relationships for determining the water temperature with a smaller amount of initial data.

In this connection it is of interest to compare the solutions obtained from these two statements of the problem, to assess the effect of the radiant energy penetrating the water on the formation of the water temperature with various intensities of turbulent exchange in the water and various water transparencies, and also to determine the conditions for which both versions yield equivalent results with the same degree of accuracy. These problems are examined by studying a deep water body with uniform density distribution /70/.

We assume that heat propagation occurs only vertically by turbulent exchange, the intensity being constant with depth. Under these conditions the vertical temperature distribution and its time variation (taking into account volume absorption of radiant energy in line with equations (5.9) and (5.10) for $\rho = \text{const}$) satisfy

$$\frac{\partial t}{\partial \tau} = k\frac{\partial^2 t}{\partial z^2} + \frac{Q(z, \tau)}{c\rho}, \text{ where } Q(z, \tau) = Q_0(\tau)\sum_{m=1}^{r} I_m \beta_m e^{-\beta_m z}. \qquad (9.1)$$

As initial data we regard as known the time variations of the following elements measured at height h_0 above the water surface: radiant energy flux I_0, effective radiation R_0 of the black surface of a pyrgeometer, air temperature t_0, wind speed v_0, and vapor pressure e_0. In this case heat balance equation (1.3) for the water surface, with allowance for expressions (3.2) and (4.4)–(4.6) governing its different components, assumes the form

$$z = 0 \quad \lambda \frac{\partial t}{\partial z} = \alpha [t - \varphi_1(\tau)], \tag{9.2}$$

where $\alpha = \alpha_0 + 4\delta\sigma T_0^3 + \alpha_q e_1 l$,

$$\varphi_1(\tau) = \frac{\alpha_0 + 4\delta\sigma T_0^3}{\alpha} t_0(\tau) - \frac{\delta R_0(\tau)}{\alpha} - \frac{\alpha_q l}{\alpha} [\bar{e} - e_0(\tau)], \tag{9.3}$$

$$\lambda = c\rho k; \quad \alpha_0 = \frac{c_p \rho_0}{\int\limits_0^{h_0} \frac{dz}{k_0(z)}}; \quad \alpha_q = \frac{0.623\rho_0}{B_0 \int\limits_0^{h_0} \frac{dz}{k_0(z)}} \tag{9.4}$$

Here B_0 is the barometric pressure, $\bar{e}$ and e_1 are coefficients in the linear relation linking the pressure of saturated vapor to temperature: $e_s = \bar{e} + e_1 t(0, \tau)$. The other notation is as before. Quantities with subscript "0" refer to the marine surface layer; quantities without a subscript refer to the water.

The second boundary condition is that at great depth the water temperature remains constant. At the initial instant the vertical temperature distribution is given in the form of a known bounded function

$$t(0, z) = f(z). \tag{9.5}$$

The solution of the stated problem can be expressed with the aid of Green's function. For a semibounded body with heat exchange on the surface

$$\begin{aligned} v(z, \xi, \tau - \eta) = {} & \frac{1}{2\sqrt{\pi k(\tau - \eta)}} \left[e^{-\frac{(z-\xi)^2}{4k(\tau-\eta)}} + e^{-\frac{(z+\xi)^2}{4k(\tau-\eta)}}\right] - \\ & - \frac{\alpha}{\lambda} e^{\frac{\alpha}{\lambda}(z+\xi) + \left(\frac{\alpha}{\lambda}\right)^2 k(\tau-\eta)} \operatorname{erfc}\left[\frac{z+\xi}{2\sqrt{k(\tau-\eta)}} + \right. \\ & \left. + \frac{\alpha}{\lambda}\sqrt{k(\tau-\eta)}\right] \end{aligned} \tag{9.6}$$

The temperature at any depth for arbitrary time is given by

$$t(z, \tau) = T(z, \tau) + \int_0^{\tau} d\eta \int_0^{\infty} \frac{Q(\eta, \xi)}{c\rho} v(z, \xi, \tau - \eta)\, d\xi, \qquad (9.7)$$

where

$$T(z, \tau) = \int_0^{\infty} f(\xi)\, v(z, \xi, \tau - \eta)\Big|_{\eta=0} d\xi +$$

$$+ k \int_0^{\tau} \varphi_1(\eta) \frac{\partial v(z, \xi, \tau - \eta)}{d\xi}\Big|_{\xi=0} d\eta. \qquad (9.8)$$

The solution for the water temperature in the second statement of the problem can be written similarly (on the assumption that the entire flux of radiant energy is absorbed at the water surface). In this case it is sufficient to assume in (9.1) that $Q(z, \tau) = 0$, and to add component $Q_0(\tau)/\alpha$ to function φ_1 in (9.2). Under these conditions

$$t'(z, \tau) = T(z, \tau) + \int_0^{\tau} \frac{Q_0(\eta)}{c\rho} \left[\frac{e^{-\frac{z^2}{4k(\tau-\eta)}}}{\sqrt{\pi k(\tau - \eta)}} - \frac{\alpha}{\lambda} \Phi_\alpha(z, \tau - \eta) \right] d\eta, \qquad (9.9)$$

where

$$\Phi_\alpha(z, \tau - \eta) = e^{\frac{\alpha}{\lambda} z + \left(\frac{\alpha}{\lambda}\right)^2 k(\tau-\eta)} \operatorname{erfc}\left(\frac{z}{2\sqrt{\pi k(\tau - \eta)}} + \right.$$

$$\left. + \frac{\alpha}{\lambda} \sqrt{(\tau - \eta) k} \right). \qquad (9.10)$$

Function $T(z, \tau)$, which describes the effect of the initial temperature distribution and heat exchange with the atmosphere by means of effective radiation, turbulent heat flux and evaporation during the formation of the temperature field in the water, is identical in both statements of the problem. We therefore examine only changes in water temperature caused by radiative heating against the background of the temperature field $T(z, \tau)$.

An explicit expression for the component in (9.7) is derived in order to quantitatively compare the solutions. If it is substituted in the expression for $Q(\xi, \tau)$ and we then integrate with respect to ξ, we obtain

$$t(z,\tau) = T(z,\tau) + \sum_{m=1}^{\nu} \frac{I_m\beta_m}{c\rho} \int_0^{\tau} Q_0(\eta) \left\{ \frac{\frac{\alpha}{\lambda}\Phi_\alpha(z,\tau-\eta)}{\frac{\alpha}{\lambda}-\beta_m} + \right.$$

$$\left. + \frac{1}{2}\Phi_\beta(-z,\tau-\eta) + \frac{1}{2}\cdot\frac{\frac{\alpha}{\lambda}+\beta_m}{\frac{\alpha}{\lambda}-\beta_m}\Phi_\beta(z,\tau-\eta) \right\} d\eta, \tag{9.11}$$

where functions Φ_β are determined by expression (9.10) with parameter $\frac{\alpha}{\lambda}$ replaced by β.

Comparison of solutions (9.9) and (9.11) shows that the first indispensable condition of their equivalence to within some degree of accuracy ε is that

$$\frac{\alpha}{\lambda\beta_m} \ll \varepsilon. \tag{9.12}$$

Here we neglect $\frac{\alpha}{\lambda}$ relative to β_m when these latter two parameters appear in the form of a sum or difference. Then the first term of the integrand in (9.11) reduces to the second term of the integrand in (9.9), where $\sum_{m=0}^{\nu} I_m = 1$. Further, if the values of β_m satisfy the inequalities

$$\beta_m \gg \frac{z}{2k\tau\sqrt{\varepsilon}} \text{ and } \beta_m \gg \frac{z}{2k\tau} + \frac{1}{\sqrt{2\varepsilon k\tau}}, \tag{9.13}$$

then the asymptotic expansion of functions Φ_β for large values of the arguments can be used and the same first terms retained to within the same degree of accuracy ε. In that case the sum of the remaining components of the integrand of (9.11) is seen not to depend on β_m and to tend toward the value of the first component of the integrand of (9.9).

Thus inequalities (9.12) and (9.13) determine the conditions under which it is possible (within some degree of accuracy ε) to neglect the effect of volume absorption of radiant energy penetrating into the water and to assume that this entire flux is completely absorbed at the surface.

For given coefficients of volume absorption, the effect of the flux of radiant energy penetrating to different depths on temperature changes decreases for a lower total coefficient of heat exchange with the atmosphere, for a higher intensity of turbulent heat exchange in the water, and for a longer computation period.

These conclusions correspond fully to the physical essence of water-temperature formation under conditions obtaining in actual water bodies. If the heat exchange at the water—air interface is small, the bulk of the heat liberated owing to radiant energy absorption is used for heating the water, and if there is intensive turbulent exchange, it propagates rapidly throughout the entire layer subjected to turbulent mixing. Under these conditions it is irrelevant where this amount of heat is liberated, whether only in the thin surface layer or throughout the entire layer of intensive turbulent mixing. However, if the turbulence is not intensive, the liberation of the same amount of heat only at the surface or distributed in depth within some layer has a different effect on the distribution of the water temperature. Equalization of the temperature in the first version of heat liberation for deep layers also requires a longer period of time, which is expressed quantitatively by inequalities (9.13).

Consider expressions (9.12) and (9.13) from the standpoint of their fulfillment under natural conditions. With mean wind speeds of 4 – 6 m/sec the total coefficient of heat exchange with the atmosphere α is of the order of 10^{-3} cal/cm^2 · sec · deg. The minimum coefficient of volume attenuation of the radiant energy is of the same order of magnitude (10^{-3} cm^{-1}). Consequently, inequality (9.12) is satisfied if $k\varepsilon \gg 1$. To within 10%, this yields turbulent exchange coefficients $k \gg 10$ cm^2/sec. Under the same conditions inequalities (9.13) are satisfied when the time intervals are longer than 5 days and the depths less than 25 m. These estimates correspond to minimum coefficients of spatial attenuation of the radiant energy. If we assume that less than half the radiant energy flux covers that part of the spectrum with such coefficients (cf. §2), the mentioned inequalities will be satisfied also when the coefficients of turbulent heat exchange in the water are smaller and the time intervals shorter.

Thus the effect of volume absorption of radiant energy on water-temperature formation is greatest when the weather is clear and calm during heating of the water when the turbulent exchange in the water is not intensive. During fall cooling, turbulent mixing in the water increases abruptly and the flux of radiant energy penetrating into the water decreases. Under these conditions inequalities (9.12) and (9.13) are almost always satisfied with an accuracy sufficient for practice, especially in regard to storage lakes and lakes where the water possesses low transparency. This enables one to disregard the volume absorption of radiant energy in the water and to study the fall cooling of lakes using a simpler statement of the problem.

These considerations can be illustrated by examining the relative effect of volume absorption of radiant energy compared with its absorption at the surface on the formation of the water surface temperature, with the aid of some mean values of the parameters appearing in (9.11). If we replace $Q_0(\eta)$ by the mean value $\overline{Q_0}$, and approximate the absorption of the entire spectrum of radiant energy penetrating into the water by some mean value $\bar{\beta}$, then integration with respect to η and substitution of $z=0$ yield

$$t(0,\tau) = T(0,\tau) + \frac{\overline{Q_0}}{c\rho}\left[1-\Phi_\alpha(0,\tau)\right]\left[1-\bar{\Phi}_{\bar{\beta}}(0,\tau)\right], \qquad (9.14)$$

where

$$\bar{\Phi}_{\bar{\beta}}(0,\tau) = \frac{\alpha}{\alpha-\lambda\bar{\beta}}\,\frac{\Phi_\beta(0,\tau)-\Phi_\alpha(0,\tau)}{1-\Phi_\alpha(0,\tau)}.$$

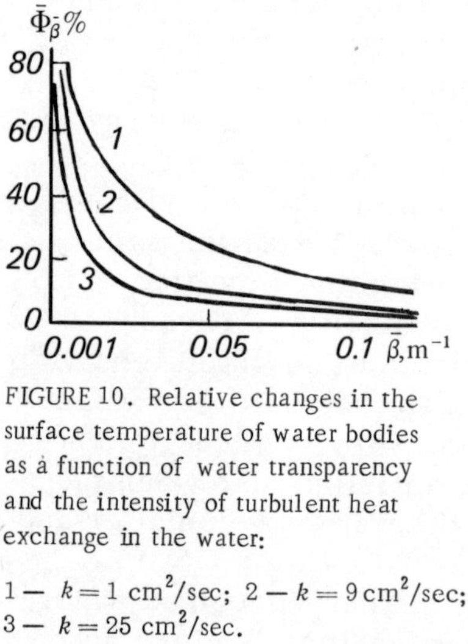

FIGURE 10. Relative changes in the surface temperature of water bodies as a function of water transparency and the intensity of turbulent heat exchange in the water:

1 — $k=1$ cm^2/sec; 2 — $k=9$ cm^2/sec; 3 — $k=25$ cm^2/sec.

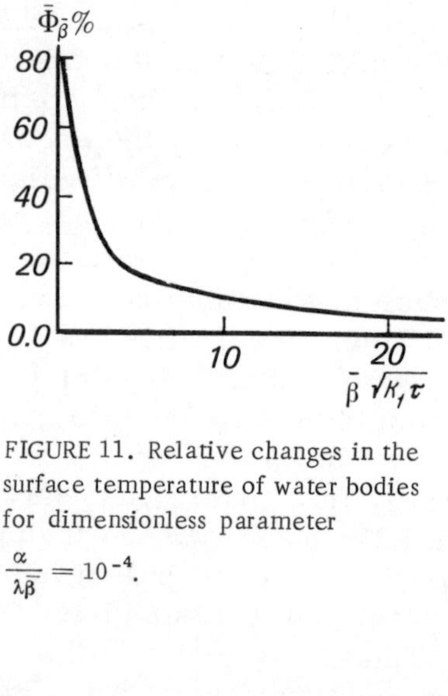

FIGURE 11. Relative changes in the surface temperature of water bodies for dimensionless parameter $\frac{\alpha}{\lambda\bar{\beta}} = 10^{-4}$.

Figures 10 and 11 illustrate the behavior of the function which determines the relative share of the changes in water-surface temperature as a result of volume absorption, when the intensity of turbulent exchange and the transparency of the water assume different values. When the turbulent exchange coefficient and the time interval are fixed, the value of $\bar{\Phi}_{\bar{\beta}}$ decreases rapidly with decreasing water transparency. An increase in turbulent exchange intensity or lengthening of the time interval have the same effect.

Calculations show that the value of $\overline{\Phi}_{\bar{\beta}}$ is insensitive to changes in dimensionless parameter $\alpha/\lambda\bar{\beta}$. When it varies between 10^{-4} and 10^{-1}, the absolute value of $\overline{\Phi}_{\bar{\beta}}$ changes by only a few percent. This allows one to determine easily, from the curve in Figure 11, the value of $\Phi_{\bar{\beta}}$ for wide ranges of values of the turbulent exchange coefficient, water transparency, and time intervals.

The general solution (9.11) can be used to show that the maximum expenditures in absolute values of temperature given by the two versions of calculating the effect of radiant energy flux refer to the surface of the water body. Expression (9.14) and the corresponding functions Φ_{β} therefore yield the largest corrections due to the volume absorption of the radiant energy and decrease fairly rapidly with depth.

In conclusion we note that the solutions obtained in (9.9) or (9.11) also yield the complete solution of the problem dealing with the distribution of water temperature and its time variation in a deep water body. To obtain solutions in explicit form and to transform them into working formulas it suffices to calculate $T(z,\tau)$, having stipulated the actual kind of initial distribution $f(z)$ and the function $\varphi_1(\tau)$ which expresses the effect of heat exchange with the atmosphere. If these functions have an arbitrary form, the integration in (9.8) cannot be carried out. But if $f(z)$ and $\varphi_1(\tau)$ are approximated by some mean values or step functions, the integrals can be easily found, and they reduce to combinations of tabulated exponential and error functions. The final expressions for the temperature distribution will not be given in these special cases.

§ 10. DIURNAL COURSE OF WATER TEMPERATURE

Diurnal or annual periodic changes resulting from the diurnal or annual course of heat exchange with the atmosphere occupy a special place in the large class of nonsteady variations in water temperature. Such fluctuations in water temperature are regular, and the fundamental regularities governing them are common to all water bodies. The amplitude and propagation depth of temperature fluctuations are determined by the range of variations in total heat exchange with the atmosphere on the surface of the water body and by the intensity of turbulent mixing in the water. Temperature waves of diurnal period affect a water layer that is between a few meters and tens of meters thick, and those of annual period in deep water bodies that do not freeze reach hundreds of meters.

Diurnal water-temperature fluctuations are most pronounced during spring and summer heating, when the weather is cloudless and calm. During the transition to fall cooling of the water the amplitude of temperature fluctuations decreases and the diurnal course is much more often distorted by other nonperiodic influences. When there is an ice cover on the water surface, it smoothes the diurnal course of water temperature, and diurnal changes occur only toward the end of the ice period when the ice becomes very transparent and thin. Under these conditions the diurnal fluctuations are determined by direct heating of the water by absorption of the sun's radiant energy penetrating through the ice.

Theoretical investigations of the diurnal course of the water temperature deal mostly with conditions in the sea. However, in view of the generality of the mathematical statement of the problem we can utilize the results of such investigations even for inland water bodies, if they are deeper than the propagation depth of the temperature fluctuations and the hydrometeorological conditions are sufficiently uniform over the area of the water body.

Schmidt was the first to investigate the propagation of temperature waves in a deep sea with uniform density. This problem was later examined by Dobroklonskii /24/ and Shtokman /90/ who aimed at computing the volume absorption of the radiant energy in the water. However, all these investigations disregarded the formation of the water-surface temperature which was previously considered a known periodic function and was not determined by the solution of the problem.

A more comprehensive statement of the problem of the diurnal course of water temperature in a uniformly dense deep sea with different initial data was obtained, in which a study of the periodic fluctuations of water temperature was based on the solution of the one-dimensional heat transfer equation subject to corresponding boundary conditions /35, 38, 41, 46/. The effect of changes in the coefficient of turbulent heat exchange with increasing depth, in the absence of volume sources, was investigated in more detail. Less attention was paid to the influence of heat sources and time variations in the coefficient of turbulent exchange on the formation of temperature fluctuations, while all treatments disregard the joint effect of these factors. The influence of nonuniform vertical distribution of density on the formation of periodic fluctuations of water temperature was not assessed either.

The problem relating to water bodies whose depth is less than the propagation depth of temperature fluctuations was investigated by Gezentsvei /21/. A numerical analysis of this problem showed that the influence of heat exchange with the bottom increases when the intensity of turbulent exchange in the water increases or when the length of the temperature wave increases; it manifests itself mainly in equalizing the temperature throughout the depth of the water body.

Consider the formation of the diurnal course of water temperature in the surface layer of a deep water body and in the marine surface layer /72/. We will assume that the heat propagates only vertically, in the atmosphere by turbulent exchange and in the water by turbulent exchange and absorption of radiant energy flux. The temperature fluctuations are assumed to be steady, and henceforth only deviations of the temperature and of the heat balance components from their mean diurnal values will be examined. The origin of coordinates is situated on the sea surface, the OZ axis being directed vertically downward to the center of the earth and the $O\xi$ axis vertically upward. All values relating to the atmosphere will be denoted by subscript 1, and those relating to the water by subscript 2.

With the formulated distribution conditions, the temperature deviations in the atmosphere and in the water and their time variations satisfy the equations

$$\text{a)}\quad \frac{\partial t_1}{\partial \tau} = \frac{\partial}{\partial \xi} k_1(\xi) \frac{\partial t_1}{\partial \xi};$$

$$\text{b)}\quad \frac{\partial t_2}{\partial \tau} = \frac{\partial}{\partial z} k_2(z) \frac{\partial t}{\partial z} + \frac{Q_0(\tau)}{c_2\rho_2} \sum_{m=1}^{\nu} I_m \beta_m e^{-\beta_m z}. \qquad (10.1)$$

The boundary conditions for this system of equations are attenuation of air and water temperature deviations at a great height in the atmosphere and at great depth in the water, temperature continuity and overall heat balance at the water–air interface:

$$z \to \infty,\ t_2 = 0;\ \xi \to \infty,\ t_1 = 0; \qquad (10.2)$$

$$z = \xi = 0,\ t_1 = t_2; \qquad (10.3)$$

$$z = \xi = 0,\ c_2\rho_2 k_2 \frac{\partial t_2}{\partial z} + c_1\rho_1 k_1 \frac{\partial t_1}{\partial \xi} + l\rho_1 k_1 \frac{\partial q_1}{\partial z} = R. \qquad (10.4)$$

Deviations in specific humidity q_1 can be determined by supplementing equations (10.1) by the equation of moisture transfer and corresponding boundary conditions:

$$\frac{\partial q_1}{\partial \tau} = \frac{\partial}{\partial \xi} k_1(\xi) \frac{\partial q_1}{\partial \xi}; \qquad (10.5)$$

$$\xi = 0\quad q_1 = q_s[t_2(0, \tau)];\quad \xi \to \infty\quad q_1 = 0, \qquad (10.6)$$

where q_s is the deviation from the mean diurnal specific humidity of saturated water vapor at temperature $t_2(0, \tau)$.

To close the statement of the problem, the nature of the changes in the turbulent exchange coefficients in the atmosphere and water must be stipulated. As a first approximation for water we assume that this coefficient is constant with depth and time. The turbulent exchange coefficient in the atmosphere is usually assumed to be a linearly increasing function of the height in the marine surface layer and constant above this layer. However, in view of the calculation of the diurnal course of the air temperature in the marine surface layer, we may confine ourselves to a rougher schematization by assuming that $k_1(\xi)$ increases linearly for the entire atmosphere:

$$k_1(\xi) = k_1(1 + \mu_1\xi), \tag{10.7}$$

where μ_1 is a parameter determined from observation data.

At present there is insufficient reliable information on the differences between the mechanisms of heat and moisture transfer in the atmosphere, and the same numerical values of the coefficients of turbulent heat and moisture exchange may be assumed. This permits the initial equations to be substantially simplified because then the distribution of atmospheric temperature and moisture are related by the simple relationship

$$q_1(\tau, \xi) = \frac{q_s(\tau)}{t_1(0, \tau)} t_1(\tau, \xi). \tag{10.8}$$

If the dependence of the specific humidity of saturated water vapor on temperature is given by the Magnus formula, the relation between the turbulent heat flux and heat exchange during evaporation takes the form

$$l\rho_1 k_1 \frac{\partial q_1}{\partial \xi}\bigg|_{\xi=0} = \mu_0 l \rho_1 k_1 \frac{\partial t_1}{\partial \xi}\bigg|_{\xi=0}, \tag{10.9}$$

where

$$\mu_0 = \frac{P_s}{P_1} \cdot \frac{10.7}{235 + \bar{t}_1}; \quad q_s = \mu_0 t_1(0, \tau). \tag{10.10}$$

Thus the equation of moisture transfer is excluded from the initial system, and the thermal effect of evaporation under the mentioned assumptions manifests itself in increased thermal capacity of the air by an amount $\mu_0 l$.

The expression for the effective radiation in the form (3.2), where (3.3) governs its deviations from the mean diurnal value, can also be expressed in terms of the water-surface temperature and the temperature gradient in the marine surface layer. If we assume that heat fluxes in the latter layer are quasi-steady and neglect the effect of diurnal moisture fluctuations, this relation has the form

$$R = b_1 t_2(0, \tau) - \frac{b_1 \ln(1 + \mu_1 h_1)}{\mu_1 F_1(\bar{q}_1)} [1 - F_1(\bar{q}_1)] \left. \frac{dt_1}{d\xi} \right|_{\xi=0}, \qquad (10.11)$$

where

$$b_1 = 4\sigma\delta T_0^3 F_1(\bar{q}_1); \quad T_0 = 273 + \bar{t}_1, \qquad (10.12)$$

$\bar{t}_1$ is the mean diurnal air temperature, $F_1(\bar{q}_1)$ is a function of the mean diurnal specific humidity, h_1 is the height within the limits of the quasi-steady heat flux.

The full heat balance (10.4) at the water surface, with allowance for expressions (10.9) and (10.11), now becomes

$$\lambda_2 \left. \frac{\partial t_2}{\partial z} \right|_{z=0} + \lambda_1 \left. \frac{\partial t_1}{\partial \xi} \right|_{\xi=0} = b_1 t_2(0, \tau), \qquad (10.13)$$

where $\lambda_2 = c_2 p_2 k_2$;

$$\lambda_1 = (c_1 + l\mu_0)\rho_1 k_1 + \frac{b_1[1 - F_1(\bar{q}_1)]}{\mu_1 F_1(\bar{q}_1)} \ln(1 + \mu_1 h_1). \qquad (10.14)$$

Thus the mathematical statement of the problem of the diurnal course of temperature deviations in the surface layer of a deep water body and in the overlying marine surface layer reduces to the solution of equations (10.1) with conditions (10.2), (10.3) and (10.13), with constant k_2, and $k_1(\xi)$ in the form (10.7).

The deviations of the flux of radiant energy $Q(\tau)$ penetrating beneath the sea surface can be expressed as a Fourier series:

$$Q_0(\tau) = \mathrm{Re} \sum_{n=1}^{\infty} A_n e^{-in\omega\tau},$$

the coefficients of which are determined by

$$A_n = \frac{1}{T} \int_{-T/2}^{T/2} Q_0(\tau) e^{+in\omega\tau} d\tau;$$

quantity T is the period of the temperature fluctuations, equal to one day.

The solution of the stated problem is sought in series form:

$$t_j = \mathrm{Re} \sum_{n=1}^{\infty} \theta_{jn} e^{-in\omega\tau} \quad (j = 1.2). \qquad (10.14a)$$

If this series is substituted into the equations and boundary conditions, we obtain a system of two ordinary equations and boundary conditions for determining the temperature wave amplitudes θ_{jn}:

$$\theta_{1n}(\xi) = \bar{\theta}_{1n}(\xi) \sum_{m=1}^{\nu} F_{n,m}(\varepsilon_{m.n}); \qquad (10.15)$$

$$\theta_{2n}(z) = \bar{\theta}_{2n}(z) \sum_{m=1}^{\nu} F_{n,m}(\varepsilon_{n,m}) + \frac{A_n}{c_2\rho_2} \sum_{m=1}^{\nu} V_{n,m}(z), \qquad (10.16)$$

where

$$\bar{\theta}_{1n}(\xi) = \frac{A_n}{D_n} H_0^{(1)}\left(a_{1n}\sqrt{i(1+\mu_1\xi)}\right);$$

$$\bar{\theta}_{2n}(z) = \frac{A_n}{D_n} H_0^{(1)}(a_{1n}\sqrt{i})\, e^{i\sqrt{i}a_{2n}z};$$

$$F_{n,m}(\varepsilon_{n,m}) = I_m(1 + i\sqrt{i}\varepsilon_{n,m})(1 + i\varepsilon^2_{n,m})^{-1};$$

$$V_{n,m} = \frac{I_m}{k_2\beta_m}\left(e^{i\sqrt{i}a_{2n}z} - e^{-\beta_m z}\right)(1 + i\varepsilon^2_{n,m})^{-1};$$

$$D_n = (b_1 - i\sqrt{i}\lambda_2 a_{2n}) H_0^{(1)}(a_{1n}\sqrt{i}) + \frac{\lambda_1\mu_1 a_{2n}\sqrt{i}}{2} H_1^{(1)}(a_{1n}\sqrt{i}); \qquad (10.17)$$

$$a_{1n} = \frac{2}{\mu_1}\sqrt{\frac{n\omega}{k_1}}, \quad a_{2n} = \sqrt{\frac{n\omega}{k_2}}, \quad \varepsilon_{n,m} = \frac{a_{2n}}{\beta_m},$$

$H_0^{(1)}$ and $H_1^{(1)}$ are Hankel functions of the first kind of zero and first order.

In these solutions functions $\bar{\theta}_{1n}$ and $\bar{\theta}_{2n}$ characterize the vertical distribution of the temperature wave amplitudes in the water and in the atmosphere, under the condition that the entire radiant energy flux is completely absorbed at the surface of the water. The effect of volume absorption of radiant energy in the water on the distribution of the temperature wave amplitudes in the atmosphere is determined by the correction factor $\sum_{m=1}^{\nu} F_{n,m}$ which does not depend on height but on the turbulence intensity in the water and on the transparency of the water masses. As regards temperature waves propagating in the water, this effect is much more complicated:

in addition to the same correction factor the solution also incorporates additional components $V_{n,m}(z)$, variable with depth and also depending on turbulence intensity in the water and on the water transparency. Substitution of function θ_{jn} $(j = 1, 2)$ into (10.14a) yields the full solution of the stated problem.

Consider changes in function $F_{n,m}$ as a function of dimensionless parameter $\varepsilon_{n,m}$, where

$$\frac{F_{n,m}}{I_m} = \bar{F}_{n,m} e^{iF'_{n,m}};$$

$$\bar{F}_{n,m} = (1 + \varepsilon^2_{n,m} - \sqrt{2}\varepsilon_{n,m})^{\frac{1}{2}} (1 + \varepsilon^4_{n,m})^{-\frac{1}{2}};$$

$$F'_{n,m} = \operatorname{arctg} \frac{\varepsilon_{n,m}}{\sqrt{2} - \varepsilon_{n,m}} - \operatorname{arctg} \varepsilon^2_{n,m}.$$

The form of $\bar{F}_{n,m}$ and $F'_{n,m}$ within the variation limits of parameter $\varepsilon_{n,m}$ is shown in Figure 12. Larger values of $\varepsilon_{n,m}$ correspond to water bodies with high water transparency and low turbulence intensity. The amplitudes of temperature fluctuations in the air over such water bodies will be considerably smaller than over water bodies with low water transparency and intensive turbulent exchange. In the latter case the formation of the air temperature over water bodies is chiefly determined by the characteristics of turbulent exchange in the water and in the atmosphere. If the condition

$$\sqrt{2}\varepsilon_{n,m} \leqslant N$$

is fulfilled, then $\bar{F}_{n,m} \longrightarrow 1$ and $F'_{n,m} \longrightarrow 0$ with degree of accuracy N. The effect of the volume absorption of radiant energy in the water on the formation of the diurnal temperature course in the atmosphere may be neglected, assuming that the entire flux of radiant energy is completely absorbed at the water surface.

Consider the change with depth of the components of the form $V_{n,m}(z)$ for the temperature wave amplitudes in the water, where

$$V_{n,m}(z) = \bar{V}_{n,m} e^{iV'_{n,m}}.$$

It can be shown that functions $\bar{V}_{n,m}$ attain a maximum at some depth below the water surface. The absolute value and the depth of this maximum is determined for each harmonic of the temperature wave by the relationship between water transparency and the intensity of turbulent exchange in the water. Figure 13 depicts changes in $\bar{V}_{n,m}$ for the first harmonic of the temperature wave as dependent on changes in the coefficient of turbulent exchange.

With increasing intensity of turbulent mixing in the water the absolute value of $\bar{V}_{n,m}$ at all depths drops abruptly, the maximum becomes less pronounced, and it attains greater depths.

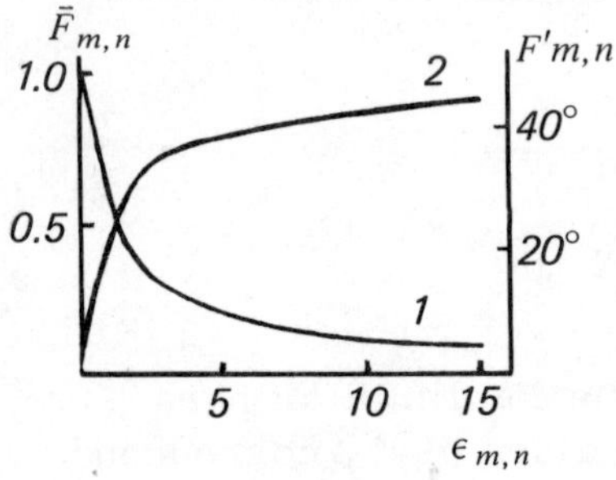

FIGURE 12. Changes in the modulus (1) and argument (2) of correction function F_{mn} as a function of water transparency and intensity of turbulent exchange.

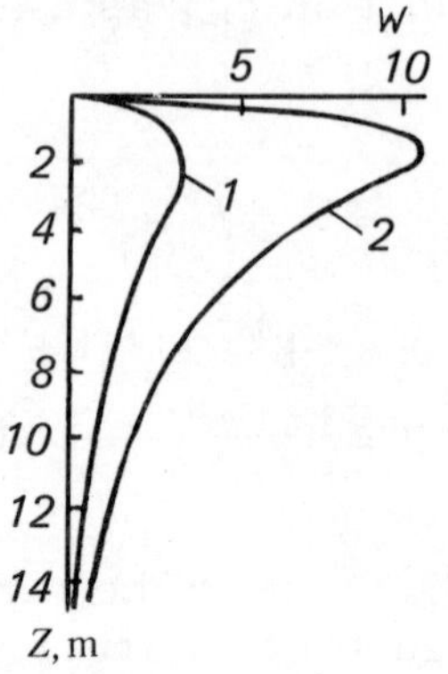

FIGURE 13. Changes with depth of the modulus of correction function W_{1m} for volume absorption of solar radiation at different intensities of turbulent heat exchange in the water.

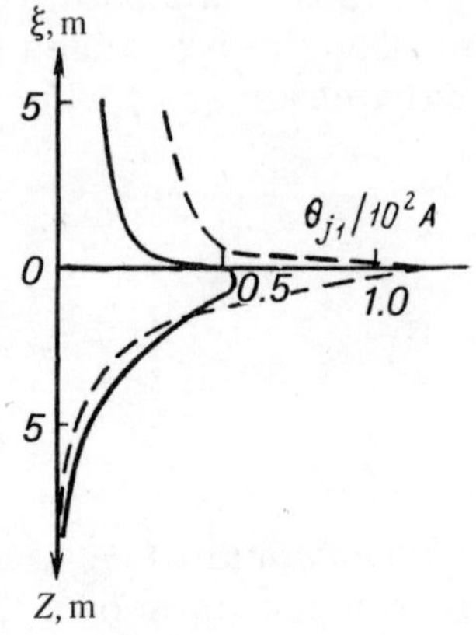

FIGURE 14. Changes in the amplitude of the first harmonic of the temperature wave in the atmosphere and in the water accounting for (——) and disregarding (-----) volume absorption of solar radiation.

Figures 14 and 15 illustrate the general solutions by presenting an example of the calculation of the amplitude and phase distribution of the first harmonic of the temperature wave in the surface layer of the water and in the marine surface layer. It is seen that the effect of volume absorption of radiant energy shows up most strongly in the temperature wave amplitude in the layers closest to the surface, and in the phase shift in deeper layers. Due to the correction for volume absorption the amplitude of temperature fluctuations at the water surface drops by almost one half, and its maximum value is attained in the first one-meter layer of water. The phase shift at the same depth reaches its minimum. In deeper layers the correction for volume absorption is small in the amplitude of the temperature wave and considerable in the phase shift. The general trend of the depth variation in amplitude and phase shift of the temperature fluctuations, calculated with allowance for volume absorption of the radiant energy of the sun in the water, agrees well with observation data. This is evident when comparing Figures 14 and 15 with Figure 16, which was plotted according to data of /19/.

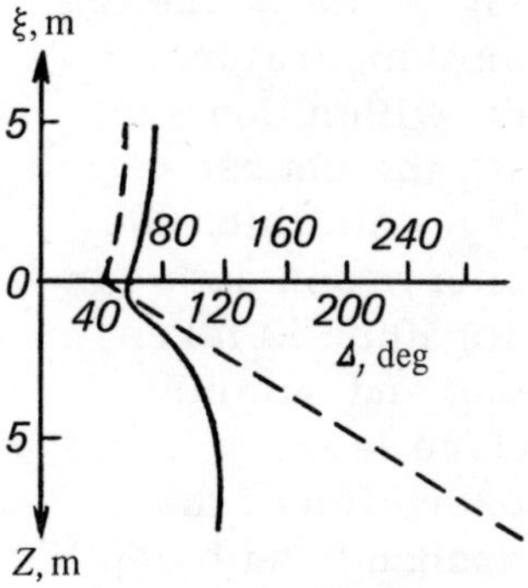

FIGURE 15. Change in the phase shift of the first harmonic of the temperature wave in the atmosphere and in the water allowing for (——) and disregarding (----) the volume absorption of solar radiation in the water.

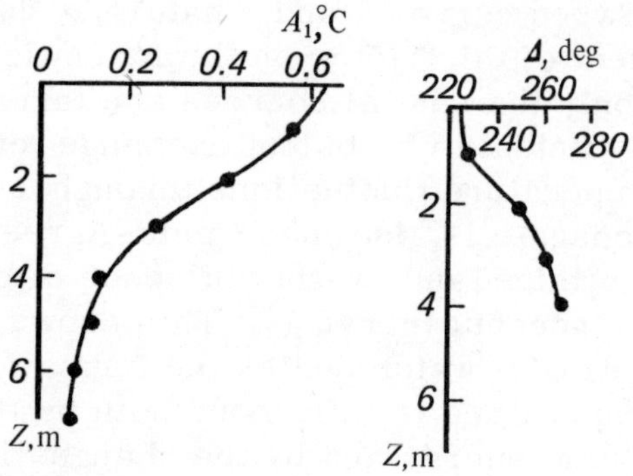

FIGURE 16. Depth variation in amplitude and phase shift of the first harmonic of the temperature wave of the daily period according to observations at the Black Sea.

Protasov /78/ solved the problem of the diurnal course of water and air temperatures stated similarly, but with a turbulent exchange coefficient that varied with depth. The first approximation for describing variations in k_2 comprised a model with the discontinuity

$$k_2 = \begin{cases} k_2' = \text{const}; \\ k_2'' = \text{const}. \end{cases} \qquad (10.18)$$

In that case the general solution is very cumbersome, and will not be computed. Numerical calculations showed that changes in k_2 with depth have a substantial effect on the amplitudes and phases of temperature waves in the atmosphere and in the water, but the above-mentioned qualitative features of the diurnal course are retained.

The combined effect of volume absorption of radiant energy and changes in turbulent exchange intensity with depth was also investigated /74/. This study is based on the solution of equation (10.1b), with k_2 selected in the form (10.18) and the given course of temperature on the water surface.

The results of this problem are compared with observation data in Figure 17. The influence both of the volume absorption of radiant energy in the water and of the change in the coefficient of turbulent exchange with depth is clear. If the first factor is neglected (curve 4), the amplitude is attenuated much more rapidly in water layers close to the surface. With increasing depth the divergence between curves 4 and 1 naturally decreases owing to the weakening effect of this factor on the formation of the water temperature. If only the spatial sources are taken into account, with a constant coefficient of turbulent exchange (curves 2 and 3), the course of temperature fluctuations throughout the entire layer in which they propagate is also incorrect. Agreement with observation data can be attained only if the influence of both factors together is taken into account (curve 1). This shows that for spring and summer heating of water bodies the formation of the surface layer temperature is influenced both by the volume absorption of the radiant energy and by the changes in turbulent exchange with depth.

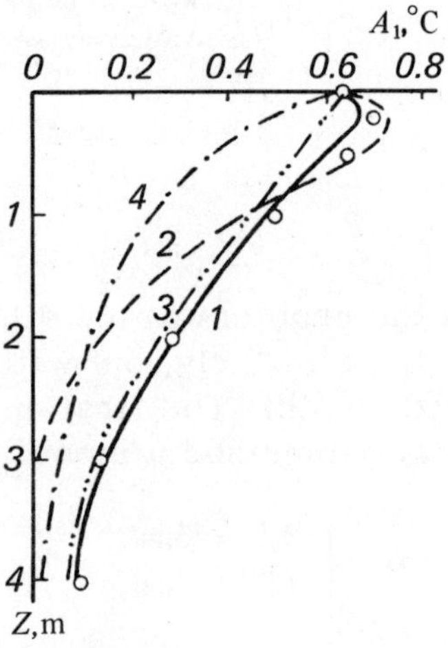

FIGURE 17. Changes in the amplitude of the first harmonic of the temperature wave of the diurnal period with depth as a function of the absorption of radiant energy and changes in the coefficient of turbulent exchange. Points indicate observation data at the Uchinskoe Reservoir.

In addition to the above-described theory of the diurnal course of water and air temperatures, another statement of the problem is often used in hydrophysical problems. In this approach the diurnal course of water temperature is examined, where the main actinometric and meteorological elements at some height in the marine surface layer or the course of the heat balance at the water surface are given. Such a statement of the problem was first formulated by Kolesnikov /38, 41/. Here the problem reduces to solving the equation of heat transfer in the water

$$\frac{\partial t_2'}{\partial \tau} = k_2 \frac{\partial^2 t_2'}{\partial z^2} + \frac{Q_0(\tau)}{c\rho} \sum_{m=1}^{\nu} I_m \beta_m e^{-\beta_m z} \quad (10.19)$$

under the condition that the total heat balance at the water surface is given. Then, in analogy to (9.2), this condition assumes the form

$$z = 0, \qquad \lambda_2 \frac{\partial t_2'}{\partial z} = \alpha [t_2' - \varphi_1'(\tau)], \quad (10.20)$$

and the condition that temperature fluctuations are attenuated at great depth.

Quantities α and $\varphi_1(\tau)$ in expression (10.20) are determined by expressions (9.3) and (9.4). Quantity α can be regarded as the total heat exchange coefficient, if there are turbulent heat and moisture fluxes and effective radiation by the water surface. Quantity $\varphi_1(\tau)$ can be regarded as some equivalent temperature expressing the influence of these components of heat exchange with the atmosphere.

If there are no measurement data pertaining to the effective radiation and specific humidity, the equivalent temperature can only be expressed in terms of the air temperature. If the heat and moisture fluxes are regarded as quasi-steady in the marine surface layer, this relation assumes the form

$$\varphi_1'(\tau) = \left(1 - \frac{b_1}{\alpha}\right) t_0(\tau),$$

where b_1 is determined by (10.12).

The solution of equation (10.19) with condition (10.20) and attenuation of temperature fluctuations at great depth in the water can be found by conventional means. The amplitude of temperature fluctuations in the water is

$$\vartheta_{2n}(z) = \frac{\alpha B_n + A_n \sum_{m=1}^{\nu} F_{n,m}}{D_n'} e^{i\sqrt{i}\, a_{2n} z} + \frac{A_n}{c_2\rho_2} \sum_{m=1}^{\nu} V_{n,m}(z), \quad (10.21)$$

$$D_n' = \alpha - i\sqrt{i}\, \lambda_2 a_{2n}, \quad (10.22)$$

where B_n is the amplitude of the fluctuations of equivalent temperature, the other notation being as before.

Comparison of the result obtained with (10.16) shows that the correction functions for volume absorption of the radiant energy in the water coincide completely in these solutions. The quantitative difference is fully determined by their first components. In general these solutions yield equivalent results if

$$\frac{\bar{A}_n H_0^{(1)}(a_{1n}\sqrt{i}) \sum_{m=1}^{\nu} F_{n,m}}{D_n} = \frac{\alpha \bar{B}_n + A_n \sum_{m=1}^{\nu} F_{n,m}}{D_n'} \qquad (10.23)$$

Assuming that the given course of the air temperature corresponds to the solution of (10.15), the coefficients in a Taylor expansion are given by the expression

$$B_n = \left(1 - \frac{b_1}{\alpha}\right) H_0^{(1)}(a_{1n}\sqrt{i(1+\mu_1 h_1)}).$$

Substitution of this expression, and the corresponding value D_n' and D_n from (10.22) and (10.17), in (10.23) yields

$$\alpha = b_1 + \frac{\lambda_1 a_{1n}\sqrt{i}\,\frac{\mu_1}{2} H_1^{(1)}(a_{1n}\sqrt{i})}{H_0^{(1)}(a_{1n}\sqrt{i}) - H_0^{(1)}(a_{1n}\sqrt{i(1+\mu_1 h_1)})}.$$

Subject to the condition that the heat and moisture fluxes in the marine surface layer are quasi-steady, we can expand the Hankel functions for small arguments. This gives the steady part of the solution for the air temperature. In such an expansion

$$\alpha = b_1 + \frac{\lambda_1 \mu_1}{\ln(1+\mu_1 h_1)}.$$

With λ_1 being given by (10.14) we obtain

$$\alpha = 4\delta\sigma(273 + \bar{t}_1)^3 + \frac{(c_1 + l\mu_0)\rho_1 k_1 \mu_1}{\ln(1+\mu_1 h_1)}.$$

The right-hand side of this expression represents the coefficient of heat exchange α given by (9.3) and (9.4), if the turbulent exchange coefficient in the atmosphere varies linearly with height in accordance with (10.17). Consequently, if the heat and moisture fluxes in the marine surface layer are quasi-steady, the solutions of (10.15) and (10.21) for the diurnal course of water temperature in the two versions of the statement yield qualitatively and quantitatively equivalent results.

§11. FALL COOLING

In investigating fall cooling of lakes and rivers, the greatest interest centers on finding a reliable computational method and of forecasting the formation of surface ice and frazil, because ice phenomena cause the greatest difficulties and disrupt the normal work of hydroengineering and hydraulic installations. However, a complete quantitative description of these phenomena is made exceedingly complicated by the phase transformation processes of water and ice, the lack of any set of measurements of the heat balance components during the period of ice-flow stoppage, and the nonexistence of a theory of crystallization of water during its turbulent mixing under natural conditions.

Ice-flow stoppage under natural conditions is preceded by a lengthy period of fall cooling of the water from the time of maximum summer temperatures until the appearance of the first ice formations. The problem of forecasting the water temperature in this period is quite determinate, its solution has an independent value, and it also yields the essential initial data for characterizing the temperature and ice regimes during ice-flow stoppage.

The duration and intensity of fall cooling of water depend on the physical geography and hydrological features of the water bodies. The main factors determining the water temperature field in this period are heat exchange with the atmosphere and with the bottom or deep waters, and also the redistribution of heat owing to turbulent mixing and currents. The general water temperature formation under these conditions was briefly examined in §7.

In the case of freshwater lakes and rivers it is useful to distinguish two periods in their fall cooling: the first from the time of maximum summer heating until fall homothermy is attained, and the second from the time of fall homothermy until the first ice forms. A characteristic feature of the first stage is the vertically nonconstant temperature stratification and mixing of water due to simultaneous action of turbulent exchange and thermal convection. In the second stage the temperature stratification is stable and prevents mixing.

For weak turbulent exchange, mixing propagates only to relatively small depths, and this permits a continuous ice cover to form on the surface while the total enthalpy of the water body is considerable. Such conditions are most likely to occur in deep lakes with low runoff, with a small surface area. As regards seas (with salinity exceeding 24.7‰), there is no such subdivision of fall cooling into two stages, because in this case the temperature of water with maximum density, until ice forms, is lower than the freezing point.

Engineering computational methods in planning the thermal conditions of storage lakes are based on the utilization of the equation of turbulent heat exchange in water; the thermal and dynamic effect of the atmosphere and the thermal effect of the bottom are allowed for by the boundary conditions. Such a statement of the problem considerably simplifies the mathematical aspect of its solution and the final theoretical relationships, but, from the physical point of view, it is considerably limited because the interaction processes at the boundaries are stipulated beforehand and are not derived in the course of solving the problem.

The main laws governing the formation of water temperature during fall cooling of shallow lakes and rivers are studied by proceeding from the following statement of the problem. We examine the cooling of the water—bottom system under the condition of full heat balance on the water surface, which indicates the thermal and dynamic effect of the atmosphere. The heat in the water and in the bottom propagates only vertically, in the water through turbulent exchange, at the bottom through molecular thermal conductivity.

As shown above, such a problem schematization indicates the main features in the formation of water temperature during fall cooling of lakes and rivers. Under these conditions the mathematical statement of the problem reduces to the simultaneous solution of the system of equations

$$\frac{\partial t_j}{\partial \tau} = k_j \frac{\partial^2 t_j}{\partial z^2} \quad (j = 2, 3)$$

with boundary conditions

$$z = 0, \quad \lambda_2 \frac{\partial t_2}{\partial z} = \alpha [t_2 - \varphi(\tau)]; \quad \varphi(\tau) = \varphi_1(\tau) + \frac{Q_0(\tau)}{\alpha},$$

$$z = h_2, \quad t_2 = t_3, \quad \lambda_2 \frac{\partial t_2}{\partial z} = \lambda_3 \frac{\partial t_3}{\partial z},$$

$$z = h_2 + h_3, \quad \lambda_3 \frac{\partial t_3}{\partial z} = 0$$

and initial condition

$$\tau = 0, \quad t_j(0, \tau) = f_j(z),$$

where h_2 and h_3 are the depth of the water body and the propagation depth of the annual temperature fluctuations below the bottom; α and $\varphi(\tau)$ are respectively the total coefficient of heat exchange with the atmosphere and the equivalent temperature, determined by relations (9.3) and (9.4); the other notation is as before. All quantities relating to water bear a subscript 2 and those relating to the bottom, subscript 3. The origin of coordinates is situated on the water surface, and the $0z$ axis is directed vertically downward.

The form of function $f_2(z)$ for the water can be stipulated according to measurement data; $f_3(z)$ for the bottom is calculated by the method of § 6.

The general solution of the problem stated can be easily derived using eigenfunctions. Such a solution was given by Kolesnikov and Pivovarov /45/, on the assumption that the coefficient of turbulent heat exchange in water is constant with increasing depth and in time. The water temperature is hence given by

$$t_2(z,\tau)=\varphi(\tau)-\varphi(0)\sum_{n=1}^{\infty}C_nZ_{2n}(z)\,e^{-\sigma_n^2\mathrm{Fo}}-$$
$$-\sum_{n=1}^{\infty}C_nZ_{2n}(z)\int_0^{\tau}\frac{\partial\varphi(\eta)}{\partial\eta}\,e^{-\sigma_n^2\left(1-\frac{\eta}{\tau}\right)\mathrm{Fo}}\,d\eta+$$
$$+\sum_{n=1}^{\infty}\frac{Z_{2n}(z)}{N_n^2}\,e^{-\sigma_n^2\mathrm{Fo}}\int_0^{h_2+h_3}g_jf_j(z)\,Z_{jn}(z)\,dz, \tag{11.1}$$

where

$$Z_{jn}(z)=\begin{cases}\cos\sigma_n\dfrac{z-h_2}{h_2}+b\,\mathrm{tg}\,d\sigma_n\sin\sigma_n\dfrac{z-h_2}{h_2} & (0\leqslant z\leqslant h_2),\\[2ex] \dfrac{\cos\sigma_n\sqrt{\dfrac{k_2}{k_3}}\,\dfrac{z-(h_2+h_3)}{h_2}}{\cos d\sigma_n} & (h_2\leqslant z\leqslant h_3+h_2),\end{cases} \tag{11.2}$$

$$N_n^2=\frac{c_2\rho_2h_2}{2}\,\frac{\sigma_n^2+\mathbf{Bi}\,(1+\mathbf{Bi})}{(\sigma_n\cos\sigma_n+\mathbf{Bi}\sin\sigma_n)^2}+\frac{c_3\rho_3h_3}{2\cos d\sigma_n},$$

$$C_n=\frac{c_2\rho_2h_2\cos\sigma_n\,(\mathrm{tg}\,\sigma_n+b\,\mathrm{tg}\,d\sigma_n)}{\sigma_n^2N_n^2},$$

$$g_j=c_j\rho_j;\quad d=\sqrt{\frac{k_2}{k_3}\,\frac{h_3}{h_2}};\quad b=\sqrt{\frac{\lambda_3c_3\rho_3}{\lambda_2c_2\rho_2}},$$

$$\mathbf{Fo}=\frac{k_2\tau}{h_2^2};\quad \mathbf{Bi}=\frac{\alpha}{\lambda_2}h_2.$$

The eigenvalue σ_n is determined by the characteristic equation, which has an infinite number of roots:

$$\frac{\sigma}{\mathbf{Bi}} = \frac{1 - b\,\mathrm{tg}\,\sigma\,\mathrm{tg}\,d\sigma}{\mathrm{tg}\,\sigma + b\,\mathrm{tg}\,d\sigma}. \tag{11.3}$$

It is evident that the laws governing the change in water temperature are determined by function $\varphi(\tau)$, indicating the effect of heat exchange with the atmosphere, and by the Fourier number **Fo**, Biot modulus **Bi**, and parameter b, which could be called the coefficient of thermal activity of the bottom in relation to the water. When $b=0$, (11.1) reduces to the solution of the problem of water cooling with heat insulation on the bottom /60/. The dimensionless quantities in (11.1) depend on the coefficient of heat exchange with the atmosphere, the intensity of turbulent mixing in the water, the depth of the water body, and the thermophysical properties of the bottom. Consider the solution obtained from the standpoint of these factors and revealing their role in the general process of fall cooling of lakes and rivers.

1. Small Biot moduli ($\mathbf{Bi} \leqslant 0.1$). For mean values $\alpha \sim 10^{-3}$ cal/cm$^2 \cdot$ sec $\cdot$ deg and $\lambda_2 \sim 10$ cal/cm $\cdot$ sec $\cdot$ deg, we find that $\mathbf{Bi} < 0.1$ corresponds to water bodies less than 10 m deep. Such conditions in reality obtain in most open water reservoirs situated in plains with a large surface area.

When the Biot number is small, the approximate minimum value of the first root of characteristic equation (11.3) is

$$\sigma_1^2 = \frac{\mathbf{Bi}}{1 + b(1 + \mathbf{Bi})\,d}. \tag{11.4}$$

All subsequent values of σ_n, with $n > 2$, are in absolute magnitude close to the roots of the equation

$$\mathrm{tg}\,\sigma + b\,\mathrm{tg}\,d\sigma = 0.$$

In view of this approximation all coefficients C_n except C_1 are close to zero, and the water temperature is not given by (11.1) but by

$$t_2'(z,\tau) = \varphi(\tau) - Z_{21}'(z)\,e^{-\sigma_1^2 \mathrm{Fo}}\Big\{C_1'\varphi(0) + C_1'\int_0^{\tau}\frac{\partial\varphi(\eta)}{d\eta}\,e^{-\sigma_1^2\frac{\eta}{\tau}\mathrm{Fo}}\,d\eta - \frac{1}{N_1^2}\int_0^{h_2+h_3} g_j f_j(z)\,Z_{1j}(z)\,dz, \tag{11.5}$$

where

$$C_1' = N_1^{-2}(c_2\rho_2 h_2 + c_3\rho_3 h_3),$$

$$N_1^2 = \frac{c_3\rho_3 h_3}{2} + \frac{c_2\rho_2 h_2}{2(1+\mathbf{Bi})^2}\left[1 + (1+\mathbf{Bi})\left(1 + \frac{c_3\rho_3 h_3}{c_2\rho_2 h_2}\right)\right],$$

and Z_{1j} is determined by (11.2) with the value of σ_1 according to (11.4).

2. **Large Biot moduli** ($\mathrm{Bi} \geqslant 100$). This case corresponds to conditions of intensive heat exchange with the atmosphere at the water surface and weak turbulent mixing in the water. In the limit $\mathrm{Bi} \longrightarrow \infty$, the water surface assumes momentarily the ambient temperature, and the mathematical statement of the problem becomes identical to the problem of cooling of the water – bottom system with a given temperature course at the surface.

When the Biot modulus is large, the roots of characteristic equation (11.3) coincide approximately with the roots of the equation

$$1 - b \operatorname{tg} \sigma \operatorname{tg} d\sigma = 0, \tag{11.6}$$

the eigenfunctions being

$$Z_{1n}^{\infty}(z) = \frac{\sin \sigma_n \dfrac{z}{h_2}}{\sin \sigma_n}. \tag{11.7}$$

Coefficients C_n^{∞} and the eigenfunctions assume respectively the form

$$C_n^{\infty} = \frac{c_2 \rho_2 h_2}{2\sigma_n N_{n,\infty}^2 \sin \sigma_n};$$

$$N_{n,\infty}^2 = \frac{c_2 \rho_2 h_2}{2} (1 + b^2 \operatorname{tg} d\sigma) + \frac{c_3 \rho_3 h_3}{2 \cos^2 d\sigma}.$$

Since the coefficient of thermal activity of the bottom $b \ll 1$, the roots of equation (11.6) are given approximately by

$$\sigma_{n,\infty} \cong (2n - 1) \frac{\pi}{2}; \tag{11.8}$$

$$d\sigma'_{n,\infty} \simeq (2n - 1) \frac{\pi}{2}. \tag{11.9}$$

For eigenvalues $\sigma'_{n,\infty}$, determined by (11.9), all values of coefficients C_n in (11.1) tend to zero, and these components may be neglected. Thus in the overall solution there remain only the components corresponding to the eigenvalues determined by (11.8). Then the eigenfunctions in (11.7) coincide with their expression corresponding to conditions of heat exchange with the soil, and coefficients C_n^{∞} differ by the constant factor

$$\frac{c_2 \rho_2 h_2 \cos^2 d\sigma_{n,\infty}}{c_2 \rho_2 h_2 [\cos^2 d \cdot \sigma_{n,\infty} + b^2 \sin^2 d \cdot \sigma_{n,\infty}] + c_3 \rho_3 h_3}. \tag{11.10}$$

Consequently, with large Biot moduli the thermal effect of the bottom on the formation of water temperature may be taken into account by a correction factor for each component of the solution. This correction factor is obtained under the assumption that there is neither heat exchange with the bottom nor additional components expressing the effect of the initial temperature distribution below the bottom. Since the correction factor (11.10) is always smaller than unity, the solution disregarding heat exchange with the bottom always yields an exaggerated cooling rate of the water. In engineering problems this yields a higher safety factor, because it speeds up the beginning and exaggerates the possible intensity of ice phenomena.

The solution of the problem assuming no heat exchange with the bottom is derived from (11.7) in the form

$$t_2^0(z,\tau)=\varphi(\tau)-\varphi(0)\sum_{n=1}^{\infty} C_n^0 Z_n^0(z)\, e^{-\sigma_{n,0}^2 \mathrm{Fo}}-$$

$$-\sum_{n=1}^{\infty} C_n^0 Z_n^0(z)\int_0^{\tau}\frac{\partial\varphi(\eta)}{\partial\tau}\, e^{-\sigma_{n,0}^2\left(1-\frac{\eta}{\tau}\right)\mathrm{Fo}}\, d\eta+$$

$$+\sum_{n=1}^{\infty} N_{n,0}^{-2} Z_n^0(z)\, e^{-\sigma_{n,0}^2 \mathrm{Fo}}\int_0^{h_2} c_2\rho_2 f_2(z)\, Z_n^0(z)\, dz, \qquad (11.11)$$

where

$$C_n^0=\frac{c_2\rho_2 h_2 \sin\sigma_{n,0}}{\sigma_{n,0}^2 N_{n,0}^2}\,;\quad Z_n^0(z)=\cos\sigma_{n,0}\,\frac{z-h_2}{h_2}\,,$$

$$N_{n,0}^2=\frac{c_2\rho_2 h_2}{2}\;\frac{\sigma_{n,0}^2+\mathbf{Bi}\,(1+\mathbf{Bi})}{(\sigma_{n,0}\cos\sigma_{n,0}+\mathbf{Bi}\sin\sigma_{n,0})^2}\,,$$

and eigenvalues $\sigma_{n,0}$ are determined from the equation

$$\mathrm{tg}\,\sigma_0=\frac{\mathbf{Bi}}{\sigma_0}\,.$$

If the Fourier number is large, the series in (11.11) converge rapidly, and in practical calculations the single first terms are sufficient.

To illustrate the application of general solutions, consider the example of computing the vertically averaged water temperature in the fall cooling of the Ivan'kovo Reservoir. The indispensable initial data are taken from observations of the meteorological island station, conducted on a raft 300 – 400 m offshore. Since there were no data on actinometric observations and during the entire period of calculation the weather was cloudy, the influence of the radiation balance of the water surface on the effective temperature was not taken into account. The total coefficient of heat exchange with the atmosphere through turbulent heat exchange and evaporative heat exchange was taken as constant. Figure 18 shows the equivalent temperatures vs. time, calculated allowing for the above-mentioned limitations. For the sake of comparison the figure also shows the air temperature and the vertically averaged water temperature vs. time. The vertically averaged water temperature follows more closely the course of the equivalent temperature, which indicates that in water temperature calculations it is indispensable to take into account the main components of heat exchange with the atmosphere.

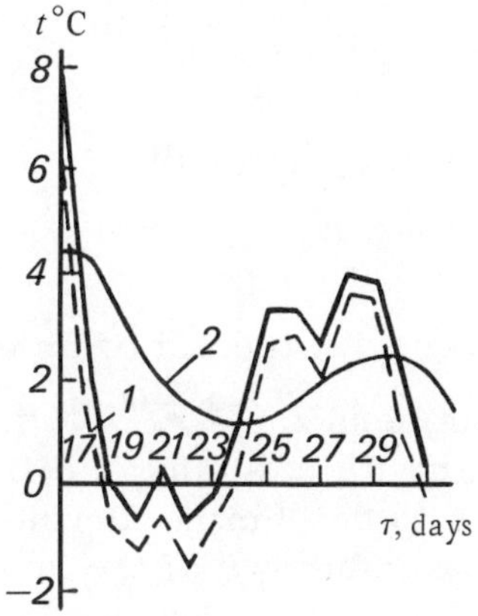

FIGURE 18. Air temperature (----), equivalent temperature (1) and vertically averaged water temperature (2) vs. time.

The method of calculating heat exchange with the bottom, explained in §6, yielded estimates of the heat flux from the bottom. In the period under consideration the heat flux was approximately two orders of magnitude smaller than the heat exchange with the atmosphere. Therefore in calculating water temperature the simpler solution omitting heat exchange with the bottom may be used as a first approximation. When the parameters (all in CGS units) have the values $\alpha = 9.5 \cdot 10^{-4}$, $c_2 = 1$, $\rho_2 = 1$, $k_2 = 5$, $h_2 = 500$, the Biot modulus $\mathbf{Bi} = 0.095$. In that case the water temperature is expressed by the simple relation (11.5) when $h_3 = 0$. Integration over the depth of the lake gives the vertically averaged water temperature in the form

$$\bar{t}_2(\tau) = \bar{t}_2(0)\, e^{-\frac{\alpha\tau}{c_2\rho_2h_2}} + \frac{\alpha}{c_2\rho_2h_2}\int\limits_0^{\tau} \varphi(\eta)\, e^{-\frac{\alpha(\tau-\eta)}{c_2\rho_2h_2}}\, d\eta. \qquad (11.12)$$

Since only discrete values $\varphi(\eta)$ of the initial data are known, this latter function is expressed in the form of a piecewise linear function:

$$\varphi(\eta) = \varphi_m + (\varphi_{m+1} - \varphi_m)\frac{\tau - ms}{s}, \quad ms \leqslant \tau \leqslant (m+1)s.$$

If we substitute this expression in (11.12) and integrate, we obtain

$$t^2(Ps) = \bar{t}_2(0)\, e^{-\frac{\alpha s}{c_2\rho_2h_2}P} + \sum_{m=0}^{P} C_k\varphi_m e^{-\frac{\alpha s(P-m)}{c_2\rho_2h_2}}, \qquad (11.13)$$

where

$$C_k = \begin{cases} C_1 = \dfrac{c_2\rho_2h_2}{\alpha s}\left(e^{\frac{\alpha s}{c_2\rho_2h_2}} - 1\right) - 1 & (m = 0), \\ C_2 = \dfrac{c_2\rho_2h_2}{\alpha s}\left(e^{-\frac{\alpha s}{c_2\rho_2h_2}} - 1\right) + 1 & (m = P), \\ C_3 = C_2 + C_1 & (1 \leqslant m \leqslant P-1). \end{cases}$$

The sum in (11.13) can be calculated with the aid of an easily constructed triangular table of the numbers $C_k e^{-\frac{\alpha s}{c_2\rho_2h_2}(P-m)}$; its rows correspond to different values of P, and its columns to different m. To compute the latter sum, it suffices to determine for the given P days the sum of the products of the numbers P of the row of the table and the row of numbers φ_m.

The results of computing the vertically averaged water temperature of the Ivan'kovo Reservoir are shown in Figure 19. It is seen that the water temperature vs. time, calculated from the equivalent temperature, coincides fairly well with observation data. A certain lowering in the rate of change of water temperature, obtained in the calculation, is clear due to neglecting the influence of the radiation balance and the depth of the reservoir. The mean depth of the section of the reservoir under consideration was taken as 5 m, whereas the water temperature was measured at depths between 3 and 4 m. Neglect of the radiation balance leads to higher equivalent temperatures during cooling and to a lower equivalent temperature while the water temperature rises. This also explains the systematic discrepancy between the courses of calculated and observed vertically averaged water temperatures. The course of water temperature calculated from air temperature is even more inertial than the actual fluctuations.

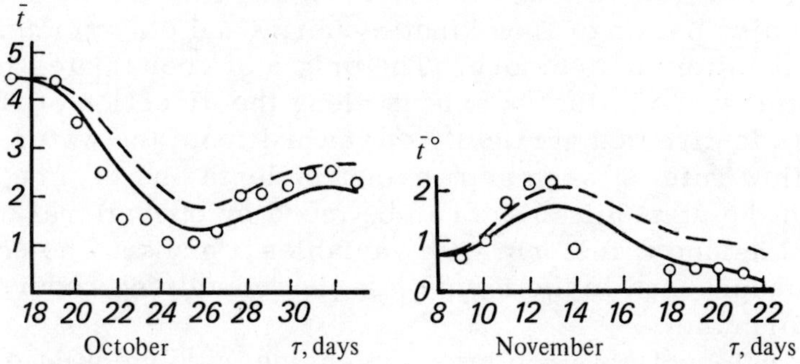

FIGURE 19. Vertically averaged water temperature vs. time, calculated from the equivalent temperature (——) and from air temperature (----). Dots indicate observation data at the Ivan'kovo Reservoir.

§12. CALCULATION OF FALL COOLING IN FLOWING WATER

The solutions examined in the foregoing section can be generalized under certain conditions to the calculation of the temperature of flowing water. If we neglect heat transfer by groundwater and horizontal temperature gradients below the bottom, the mathematical statement of the problem, with allowance for heat advection by flow and vertical turbulent mixing in the water, amounts to solving the system of equations

$$\frac{\partial t_2}{\partial \tau} + v_2 \frac{\partial t_2}{\partial x} = k_2 \frac{\partial^2 t_2}{\partial z^2} + \frac{q_2}{c_2 \rho_2}\,; \quad \frac{\partial t_3}{\partial \tau} = k_3 \frac{\partial^2 t_3}{dz^2} \tag{12.1}$$

with boundary conditions

$$z = 0, \quad \lambda_2 \frac{\partial t_2}{\partial z} = \alpha\,[t_2 - \varphi(\tau)],$$

$$z = h_2, \quad t_2 = t_3, \; \lambda_2 \frac{\partial t_2}{\partial z} = \lambda_3 \frac{\partial t_3}{\partial z}\,, \tag{12.2}$$

$$z \to \infty, \quad t_3 = \theta_3 = \mathrm{const}$$

and initial conditions

$$\tau = 0, \quad t_j = f_j(z, x) \quad (j = 2, 3),$$
$$x = 0, \quad t_2 = \psi_2(z, \tau), \tag{12.3}$$

where v_2 is the flow rate of the water, q_2 are internal heat sources due to the dissipation of flow kinetic energy and other factors, and the other notation is as before. The origin of coordinates is situated on the water surface, the $0x$ axis is along the direction of flow, and the $0z$ axis is directed vertically downward from the water surface.

If the flow rate is taken as constant in depth and in time, the solution of the stated problem can be found by operational calculus, using the Laplace transform with variables x and τ. The solution is generally expressed in the form of series containing recurrent integral formulas.

For many practical problems and engineering calculations it is sufficient to know the vertically averaged water temperature, especially since deviations in the vertically averaged water temperature from the actual temperature are very small at various depths during fall cooling of relatively shallow storage lakes. We therefore examine the approximate solution of the problem with allowance for heat advection, yielding simple theoretical relationships for determining the vertically averaged water temperature vs. time.

Integration of the first of equations (12.1) over the water depth from the surface to the bottom gives

$$c_2\rho_2 h_2\left[\frac{\partial \bar{t}_2}{\partial \tau} + \bar{v}_2\frac{\partial \bar{t}_2}{\partial x}\right] = -c_2\rho_2\left(k_2\frac{\partial t_2}{\partial z}\right)_0 + $$
$$+ c_2\rho_2\left(k_2\frac{\partial t_2}{\partial z}\right)_{h_2} + \bar{q}_2 h_2, \tag{12.4}$$

where $\bar{v}_2$ is the vertically averaged flow rate of the water,

$$\bar{t}_2 = \frac{1}{h_2}\int_0^{h_2} t_2(x, z, \tau)\,dz; \quad \text{and}\ \bar{q}_2 = \frac{1}{h_2}\int_0^{h_2} q_2(x, \tau, z)\,dz$$

are the vertically averaged water temperature $\bar{t}_2$ and enthalpy $\bar{q}_2$ due to the existence of internal sources.

We introduce conversion factors μ_2 and μ_3 from the surface and bottom temperatures, respectively, to the mean temperature. During fall cooling of relatively shallow storage lakes these coefficients are close to unity. A similar method introducing coefficient μ_2 was used by Timofeev /86/ to calculate the surface temperature of storage lakes. Taking μ_2 into account, the first term of (12.4) is determined from the boundary condition on the water surface,

$$-c_2\rho_2\left(k_2\frac{\partial t}{\partial z}\right)_0=\alpha\,[\mu_2\bar{t}_2-\varphi(\tau)]. \tag{12.5}$$

The heat flux from the bottom is found by solving the second equation of system (12.1), with boundary condition

$$z=h_2,\quad t_3=\mu_3\bar{t}_2(x,\tau) \tag{12.6}$$

pertaining to the boundedness of the temperature at great depth and initial condition (12.3). The solution of such a problem is

$$t_3(z,\tau)=\frac{1}{2\sqrt{\pi k_3\tau}}\int\limits_{h_2}^{\infty}f_3(\xi)\,[e^{-\frac{(z-h_2-\xi)^2}{4k_3\tau}}-e^{-\frac{(z-h_2-\xi)^2}{4k_3\tau}}]\,d\xi+$$

$$+\frac{\mu_3(z-h_2)}{2\sqrt{\pi k_3}}\int\limits_0^{\tau}\bar{t}_2(x,\eta)\,\frac{e^{-\frac{(z-h_2)^2}{4k_3(\tau-\eta)}}}{(\tau-\eta)^{3/2}}\,d\eta.$$

Differentiation of this expression with respect to z and multiplication by the thermal conductivity coefficient λ_b of the bottom yields the heat flux. For $z=h_2$, this gives the second component in the right-hand part of (12.4). Thus the vertically averaged water temperature satisfies the integrodifferential equation

$$\frac{\partial\bar{t}_2}{\partial\tau}+\bar{v}_2\frac{\partial\bar{t}_2}{\partial x}=-\frac{\alpha}{c_2\rho_2h_2}[\mu_2\bar{t}_2-\varphi(\tau)]+\frac{\bar{q}_2}{c_2\rho_2}+$$

$$+\frac{c_3\rho_3}{2c_2\rho_2h_2\sqrt{\pi k_3\tau}}\int\limits_{h_2}^{\infty}\xi f_3(\xi)\,e^{-\frac{\xi^2}{4k_3\tau}}\,d\xi+$$

$$+\frac{c_3\rho_3\sqrt{k_3}\mu_3}{2c_2\rho_2h_2\sqrt{\pi}}\int\limits_0^{\tau}\frac{\bar{t}_2(\eta)}{(\tau-\eta)^{3/2}}\,d\eta. \tag{12.7}$$

A similar statement of the problem and its solution for the vertically averaged water temperature was examined previously /48, 49/. One solution is given /49/ for lakes without runoff ($\bar{v}_2=0$). Another work /48/ takes heat advection by flow into account, and the boundary condition on the surface of the bottom soil is taken, instead of (12.6), in the form of the coefficient of heat exchange between the water and bottom multiplied by the difference between the bottom temperature and the vertically averaged water temperatures. Such a condition does not introduce any fundamental changes, but it makes the final relationships in the calculation much more complicated. We therefore consider the solution of equation (12.7) as more convenient in practical calculations.

Consider the Laplace transform with respect to the variable τ as applied to (12.7). Then, with allowance for the initial distribution of temperature $\bar{t}_2(0, x)$ in the water in the region of the transform, we obtain

$$\bar{v}_2 \frac{dT_2}{dx} + D(p) T_2 = F(x, p), \tag{12.8}$$

where

$$D(p) = \bar{a}\sqrt{p} + p + \bar{b},$$

$$F(x, p) = \bar{t}_2(0, x) + \frac{c_3\rho_3}{c_2\rho_2 h_2} \int_{h_2}^{\infty} f_3(\xi)\, e^{-\sqrt{\frac{p}{k_3}}\,\xi}\, d\xi +$$

$$+ \frac{1}{c_2\rho_2}\left[Q_2 + \frac{\alpha}{h_2}\Phi(p)\right], \quad \bar{a} = \frac{c_3\rho_3\mu_3\sqrt{k_3}}{c_2\rho_2 h_2},$$

$$\bar{b} = \frac{\alpha\mu_2}{c_2\rho_2 h_2}, \quad T_2(x, p) = \int_0^{\infty} e^{-p\tau}\bar{t}_2(x, \tau)\, d\tau. \tag{12.9}$$

The solution of this equation, with initial condition $T_2 = T_2'(0, p)$ at $x = 0$, is

$$T_2(x, p) = \frac{F(x, p)}{D(p)} + \left[T_2'(0, p) - \frac{F(0, p)}{D(p)}\right] e^{-D(p)x/\bar{v}_2} -$$

$$- \frac{1}{D(p)} \int_0^x \frac{\partial F(p, \eta)}{\partial \eta}\, e^{-D(p)(x-\eta)/\bar{v}_2}\, d\eta. \tag{12.10}$$

The first term of this expression describes changes in the vertically averaged water temperature when $\bar{v}_2 = 0$. It coincides fully with the solution for a lake without runoff /49/. The transform $1/D(p)$ corresponds to the inverse transform

$$\frac{1}{D(p)} \rightarrow \psi_0(\tau) = \sum_{n=1}^{2} \frac{p_n + \bar{b} - \bar{a}\sqrt{p_n}\,\mathrm{erf}\sqrt{p_n\tau}}{2(p_n + \bar{b}) - \bar{a}^2}\, e^{p_n\tau}, \tag{12.11}$$

where

$$p_1 = -\frac{2\bar{b} - \bar{a}^2}{2} + \frac{\bar{a}}{2}\sqrt{\bar{a}^2 - 4\bar{b}},$$

$$p_2 = -\frac{2\bar{b} - \bar{a}^2}{2} - \frac{\bar{a}}{2}\sqrt{\bar{a}^2 - 4\bar{b}}. \tag{12.12}$$

All the other terms of (12.10) express the influence of heat advection by flow on the formation of the water temperature.

The inverse transforms of these terms can also be derived using tables and properties of Laplace transforms. Hence

$$\Psi_1(p) = \frac{1}{p} e^{-D(p)x/\bar{v}_2} \doteq \begin{cases} \psi_1(\tau, x) & \text{for } \tau > \dfrac{x}{\bar{v}_2}, \\ 0 & \text{for } \tau < \dfrac{x}{\bar{v}_2}, \end{cases} \quad (12.13)$$

$$\psi_1(x, \tau) = e^{-\bar{b}x/\bar{v}_2}\left[1 - \operatorname{erf}\frac{\bar{a}x}{2\bar{v}_2\sqrt{\tau}}\right]. \quad (12.14)$$

Application of the convolution theorem gives

$$\frac{1}{pD(p)} e^{-D(p)x/\bar{v}_2} \doteq \begin{cases} \psi_2(x, \tau) & \text{for } \tau > \dfrac{x}{\bar{v}_2}, \\ 0 & \text{for } \tau < \dfrac{x}{\bar{v}_2}, \end{cases} \quad (12.15)$$

$$\psi_2(x, \tau) = \int\limits_0^{\tau - x/\bar{v}_2} \psi_0(\eta)\,\psi_1(\tau - x/\bar{v}_2 - \eta)\, d\eta. \quad (12.16)$$

These expressions show that the general solution for the water temperature differs when $\tau < x/\bar{v}_2$ and $\tau > x/\bar{v}_2$. In the former case, upon transition to the inverse transform all the terms of (12.10), except the first, vanish. That means that the formation of the water temperature at point x when $\tau < x/\bar{v}_2$ does not depend on the flow rate and is the same as in lakes without runoff. The influence of advective transfer must be assumed to begin only at times $\tau > x/\bar{v}_2$.

In analogy with theoretical investigations of air mass transformation /3/, the advection of heat in water can be interpreted like the movement of some front whose influence on the water temperature makes itself felt only after it has extended beyond the examined point x.

Variations in water temperature at times $\tau > x/\bar{v}_2$ can be illustrated by expressing the solution of the problem without taking into account heat exchange with the bottom. In the period of fall cooling this heat exchange represents only a slight correction and may be neglected in the first approximation. If we further assume that the vertically averaged water temperature in the discharge does not change with time, and that the temperature at the initial instant and the components of heat exchange with the atmosphere are constant along the investigated section, the solution assumes the very simple form

$$\bar{t}_2(x, \tau) = \bar{t}_2(0) e^{-\bar{b}x/\bar{v}_2} + \frac{1}{c_2\rho_2} \int\limits_{\tau - x/\bar{v}_2}^{\tau} \left[q_2 + \frac{\alpha}{h_2}\varphi(\eta)\right] e^{-\bar{b}(\tau-\eta)} d\eta. \quad (12.17)$$

There is no difficulty in deriving the inverse transform at time $\tau > x/\bar{v}_2$, even in the general case of equation (12.10). Each term of this equation may be considered as the product of two transforms whose inverse transforms are known either from the conditions of the problem or from relations (12.11) through (12.16). Application of the theorem dealing with the multiplication of transforms to each term also yields the general solution of the problem. However, the resulting general expressions are fairly cumbersome and inconvenient for analyzing and calculating changes in water temperature. Besides, this method of obtaining an exact solution does not allow one to take into account length and time changes in thermal and hydrological parameters.

Consider a solution of equation (12.7) which is approximate, but free from these limitations. This solution is based on the present author's work /71/ and can be generalized to fall cooling of water. We divide the water body along its length into a number of sections with approximately equal hydrological conditions. As an approximation it is assumed that the vertically averaged water temperature within each section can be approximated by the linear function

$$\bar{t}_{2,j}(x, \tau) = \bar{t}_{2,j}(\tau) + \frac{x - x_j}{x_{j+1} - x_j}(\bar{t}_{2,j+1} - \bar{t}_{2,j}). \qquad (12.18)$$

Function $\bar{t}_{2,j}$, describing time variations in temperature for the runoff of the lake or at the beginning of section j, is known only from the initial condition when $x=0$ or as a result of calculating the water temperature at the end of section $j-1$. The solution of the problem thus amounts to determining the course of the temperature at the end of section $j+1$.

We represent the course of the water temperature at the end of section $j+1$ in the form of a step function:

$$t_{2,j+1} = \psi_m + (\psi_{m+1} - \psi_m)\frac{\tau - ms}{s} \quad (ms \leqslant \tau \leqslant (m+1)s), \qquad (12.19)$$

and this enables us to obtain in explicit form the integral in the last term on the right-hand side of (12.7). Substitution of (12.19) in (12.7) and integration of the latter with respect to time over time interval ν yields

$$\bar{t}_{2,\nu} = M_\nu t_{2,\nu-1} + \frac{4}{3}\sqrt{\frac{s}{\pi}}\,\frac{\sqrt{\lambda_3 c_3 \rho_3 \mu_3}}{c_2 \rho_2 h_2 N_\nu}\sum_{m=0}^{\nu-1}\bar{t}_{2,m}\Phi_{m,\nu} + F(x, \nu s), \qquad (12.20)$$

where

$$F(x, \nu s) = \frac{1}{c_2\rho_2 h_2 N_\nu} \int\limits_{(\nu-1)s}^{\nu s} \Big\{ \alpha\varphi(x, \tau) + h_2 q_2(x, \tau) + \frac{c_3\rho_3}{2\sqrt{\pi k_3 \tau^3}} \int\limits_{h_2}^{\infty} \xi f_3(\xi) e^{-\frac{\xi^2}{4k_3\tau}} d\xi + \frac{c_2\rho_2 h_2 \bar{v}_2}{x - x_j} \bar{t}_{2,j}(\tau) \Big\} d\tau; \qquad (12.21)$$

$$M_\nu = \frac{1}{N_\nu}\left(1 - \frac{\alpha s}{c_2\rho_2 h_2} - \frac{\bar{v}_2 s}{x_{j+1} - x_j}\right); \qquad (12.22)$$

$$N_\nu = 1 + \frac{1}{2}\left(\frac{\alpha s}{c_2\rho_2 h_2} + \frac{\bar{v}_2 s}{x_{j+1} - x_j}\right) + \frac{4}{3}\sqrt{\frac{s}{\pi}} \frac{\sqrt{\lambda_3 c_3 \rho_3}}{c_2\rho_2 h_2} \mu_3;$$

$$\Phi_0 = \nu^{3/2} - 2(\nu - 1)^{3/2} + \frac{3}{2}(\sqrt{\nu} - \sqrt{\nu - 1}); \qquad (12.23)$$

$$\Phi_{m,\nu} = 3(\nu - m)^{3/2} - 3(\nu - m - 1)^{3/2} + (\nu - m - 2)^{3/2} - (\nu - m + 1)^{3/2}.$$

This expression determines the vertically averaged water temperature at times $\tau = \nu s$ as a function of its values at the preceding instants of time and also of the thermal and hydrological conditions of section j of the lake. (For the sake of brevity subscript j is omitted in (12.20) and henceforth.) Successive application of expression (12.20) in time or for adjacent sections makes it possible to calculate the total change in water temperature. Thermal and hydrological parameters of the lake appearing in the solution are taken as constant only within the limits of interval ν or of section j, and they may change jumpwise upon transition from one interval or section to another. If the parameters have fixed values, the solution of (12.20) makes it possible to easily assess quantitatively the influence of various factors determining the formation of the water temperature.

TABLE 7. Functions $\Phi_{m,\,\nu} \cdot 10^3$ for calculating the vertically averaged water temperature

ν	m = 0	1	2	3	4	5	6	7	8
2	207	172							
3	63.4	289	172						
4	34.2	103	289	172					
5	22.4	59.6	103	289	172				
6	16.1	40.2	59.6	103	289	172			
7	12.3	29.5	40.2	59.6	103	289	172		
8	9.82	22.9	29.5	40.2	59.6	103	289	172	
9	8.07	18.4	22.9	29.5	40.2	59.6	103	289	172
10	6.77	15.2	18.4	22.9	29.5	40.2	59.6	103	289
11	5.89	12.9	15.2	18.4	22.9	29.5	40.2	59.6	103
12	5.02	11.1	12.9	15.2	18.4	22.9	29.5	40.2	59.6
13	4.43	6.63	11.1	12.9	15.2	18.4	22.9	29.5	40.2
14	3.92	8.51	6.63	11.1	12.9	15.2	18.4	22.9	29.5
15	3.53	7.57	8.51	6.63	11.1	12.9	15.2	18.4	22.9
16	3.17	6.81	7.57	8.51	6.63	11.1	12.9	15.2	18.4
17	2.88	6.16	6.81	7.57	8.51	6.63	11.1	12.9	15.2
18	2.64	5.61	6.16	6.81	7.57	8.51	6.63	11.1	12.9
19	2.42	5.13	5.61	6.16	6.81	7.57	8.51	6.63	11.1
20	2.23	4.72	5.13	5.61	6.16	6.81	7.57	8.51	6.63
21	2.07	4.36	4.72	5.13	5.61	6.16	6.81	7.57	8.51
22	1.93	4.05	4.36	4.72	5.13	5.61	6.16	6.81	7.57
23	1.78	3.76	4.05	4.36	4.72	5.13	5.61	6.16	6.81
24	1.68	3.52	3.76	4.05	4.36	4.72	5.13	5.61	6.16
25	1.58	3.29	3.52	3.76	4.05	4.36	4.72	5.13	5.61
26	1.48	3.05	3.29	3.52	3.76	4.05	4.36	4.72	5.13
27	1.40	2.91	3.05	3.29	3.52	3.76	4.05	4.36	4.72
28	1.32	2.75	2.91	3.05	3.29	3.52	3.76	4.05	4.36
29	1.25	2.61	2.75	2.91	3.05	3.29	3.52	3.76	4.05
30	1.19	2.46	2.61	2.75	2.91	3.05	3.29	3.52	3.76
31	1.13	2.34	2.46	2.61	2.75	2.91	3.05	3.29	3.52
32	1.08	2.23	2.34	2.46	2.61	2.75	2.91	3.05	3.29
33	1.03	2.12	2.23	2.34	2.46	2.61	2.75	2.91	3.05
34	0.99	2.02	2.12	2.23	2.34	2.46	2.61	2.75	2.91
35	0.95	1.92	2.02	2.12	2.23	2.34	2.46	2.61	2.75

There is no difficulty in the practical application of (12.20) for calculating the vertically averaged water temperature. The integrals in (12.21) can be replaced by the mean values of the corresponding functions for interval ν. Function $\Phi_{m,\nu}$ can be easily tabulated, and since it does not depend on the physical parameters, tabulated values of this function are universal. Table 7 represents such a table for $\nu = 35$. Calculation of water temperature at any section, using the table of functions $\Phi_{m,\,\nu}$, can be easily standardized. Application of this method in actual calculations is illustrated by the example of forecasting water temperatures beneath ice.

Chapter III

THE WINTER TEMPERATURE REGIME

§13. GENERAL STATEMENT OF THE PROBLEM AND ITS SCHEMATIZATION

By the thermal winter regime of freezing lakes and rivers we mean the period from the establishment of a continuous ice cover on the surface to its breakup (§ 7). The basis for such a definition is the fact that there is a substantial difference in the role of heat exchange with the atmosphere during the formation of the water temperature in the presence or absence of a continuous ice cover on the surface of the water body.

In the ice-free period the fundamental laws governing changes in water temperature are determined by heat exchange with the atmosphere on the open surface of water, while heat exchange with the bottom or lower lying groundwater is a kind of correction factor.

The relationship between these processes is entirely different in the ice period: the total heat exchange with the atmosphere by turbulent exchange, evaporation, and effective radiation is replaced by the heat flux through the ice and snow. On the underside of the ice cover the ice-formation processes cause the temperature to remain constant and equal to the freezing point. The thermal effect of the atmosphere results mainly in the buildup or thawing of the ice cover, but it causes practically no changes in water temperature, except when the ice is thin and transparent and there is no snow. Heat exchange with the bottom or groundwater becomes the decisive external factor in the formation of the water temperature of ice-covered water bodies.

The rate of heat transport from the bottom to the underside of the ice is determined by turbulent exchange in the water. The intensity of this exchange in winter is substantially smaller than during fall cooling, because the continuous ice cover excludes such an important factor as mixing due to wind. Heat convection in freshwater lakes is also impeded by a stable temperature stratification. The main causes of turbulent mixing in actual lakes are and remain currents and uneven depth.

The general outlines and qualitative features of the course of water temperature under the ice cover in winter were reviewed briefly in §7. The task of a quantitative theory is to develop a method of forecasting this temperature course at different depths during the entire ice period and to work out methods of computing or forecasting the processes governing the buildup and thawing of the ice. The necessity of solving these problems is dictated by practical questions of designing and operating various kinds of hydroengineering and hydraulic installations. Forecasting water temperature beneath ice throughout winter, from initial data pertaining to the time a continuous ice cover is established, is possible because the thermal conditions of the atmosphere have only a slight effect on the formation of the temperature field in the water. The solution of this problem is in itself important, but in addition it yields the essential initial data for solving problems of the ice regime of storage lakes and of tailraces (cf. §20).

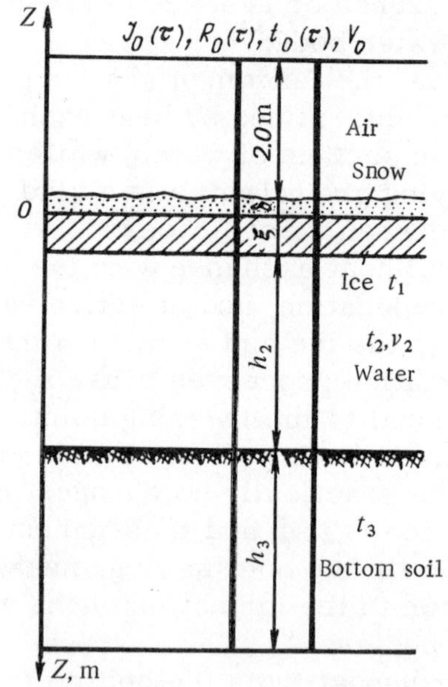

FIGURE 20. Illustration pertaining to the statement of the problem of the winter thermal conditions in lakes and rivers.

The general mathematical statement of the problem dealing with the winter thermal conditions of freezing lakes and rivers is a one-dimensional problem concerning heat transfer in a four-layer medium (snow – ice – water – bottom), presented in Figure 20. Thus the problem is reduced to the simultaneous solution of a system of equations for such a multilayered medium with boundary conditions at the snow – ice and water – bottom interfaces, the condition of full heat balance at the snow surface, the conditions that the temperature be equal to zero and the balance equation of ice formation on the lower surface of the ice be equal to zero, and the condition of constant temperature at some depth in the bottom soil (Kolesnikov).

Initial data comprise the known course of the main actinometric and meteorological elements at some altitude in the air above the snow and the initial temperature distribution in all the media: the thermal characteristics of the adjacent media and the turbulent exchange in air and water. Thus stated, the problem is mathematically closed and its solution would provide a complete notion of the formation of winter thermal conditions in freezing lakes and rivers.

However, the analytical solution of such a problem with a movable water – ice interface, even subject to the condition of steady heat fluxes in the ice and snow covers, is mathematically very difficult. Besides, the solution would require a considerable number of parameters and initial data that are not known with sufficient accuracy. It is therefore expedient and justifiable to simplify the general statement of the problem by dividing it into two. This is justified by the slight influence of the thermal conditions of the atmosphere on changes in water temperature under the ice, and also by the slow shift of the water – ice interface and the small changes in lake depth owing to the shift of this interface.

The first problem deals with the thermal conditions of the water – soil system, and the second with the buildup or thawing of the ice for a known heat flux from the water to the ice.

At first, the methods of forecasting the water temperature under the ice cover were developed disregarding heat exchange with the bottom, and therefore the relationships used in the calculations were not sufficiently reliable and in agreement with measurement data. A critical review of such methods is contained in papers by Vereshchagin /18/ and Korytnikova /57/.

Present methods of forecasting water temperature under ice take into account heat exchange with the bottom as one of the basic factors. However, it is not determined on the basis of a simultaneous examination of the formation of the temperature field in the water – bottom system, but is regarded as previously known for the entire winter. When thus stated, the water temperature is determined by solving the heat transfer equation in water with constant (zero) temperature at the water – ice interface, stipulated by the heat flux at the water – bottom interface and corresponding to the initial conditions in water /6, 58/.

Changes in heat flux from the bottom are calculated variously by these methods according to the course of the near-bottom water temperatures (§6). However, regardless of how the heat exchange with the bottom is calculated, methods of forecasting water temperature in engineering calculations have one fundamental shortcoming. When these methods are applied, the course of the near-bottom water temperature must be stipulated in advance, but for the winter period this is actually a sought function and it cannot be determined accurately when the heat flux from the bottom is not known. As a way out it is proposed to use actual measurements of near-bottom temperatures in analogous lakes or to proceed in the calculation by successive approximations. However, since we then lack a criterion to ascertain correct selection of the curve of the course of near-bottom temperatures, it is not possible to rigorously assess the accuracy of the forecast water temperature.

If the main laws governing the formation of the water temperature under the ice cover are to be described with sufficient reliability, the thermal conditions of the water — bottom system must be examined jointly. Such a statement of the problem amounts mathematically to the simultaneous solution of the system of equations of heat transfer in water and below the bottom, with corresponding boundary and initial conditions. Various solutions have been examined /39, 40, 56, 68, 69/. All these works have in common the assumption that there is no advective heat transfer. They all neglect changes in lake depth owing to the buildup or thawing of ice, and they assume that the temperature at the water — ice interface is equal to zero throughout the winter.

The main difference is in the selection of the boundary condition at some depth below the bottom (Kolesnikov) or taking the bottom as a semi-infinite medium (Korytnikova and Pivovarov). The stipulation of this boundary condition determines the mathematical method of solving the problem and the final explicit form of the solution. The methods of forecasting water temperature under ice and the heat flux from the water at the underside of the ice cover, proposed in these works, are sufficiently general and do not present any difficulties when applied in practice.

A brief survey and solution of the second problem of the winter thermal conditions of lakes and rivers, especially the problem of the buildup and thawing of ice, are given in §16.

§14. THE TEMPERATURE REGIME OF WATER UNDER ICE COVER

We now give a mathematical statement of water temperature formation under ice cover for the accepted schematization of the general statement of the problem dealing with winter thermal conditions of freezing lakes and rivers. Consider a water body of depth h_2 with horizontally uniform thermal and hydrological conditions, and isolate a water column of unit cross-section and height h_2 and an adjoining column of the bottom. The origin of coordinates is situated on the water — ice interface, and the $0z$ axis is directed vertically downward. We assume that heat propagation in the water is effected by turbulent exchange, and in the bottom soil by molecular thermal conductivity. Under these conditions the temperature distribution in the water and below the bottom is determined by the system of equations

$$\frac{\partial t_j}{\partial \tau} = k_j \frac{\partial^2 t_j}{\partial z^2} \quad (j = 2, 3). \tag{14.1}$$

Henceforth all quantities relating to water carry subscript 2; those relating to the bottom carry subscript 3.

The boundary conditions comprise: zero temperature at the water — ice interface,

$$z = 0, \quad t_2 = 0; \tag{14.2}$$

a matching condition at the water — bottom interface,

$$z = h_2, \quad t_2 = t_3, \quad \lambda_2 \frac{\partial t_2}{\partial z} = \lambda_3 \frac{\partial t_3}{\partial z}; \tag{14.3}$$

and either the condition that the temperature at the propagation depth of annual temperature fluctuations is constant (Kolesnikov),

$$z = h_2 + h_3, \quad t_3 = \theta_3, \tag{14.4}$$

or the condition of boundedness at infinity (Korytnikova and Pivovarov),

$$z \to \infty, \quad t_3 = \theta_3. \tag{14.5}$$

The initial time is when a continuous ice cover forms on the water surface. At that time the temperature distribution in the water and in the bottom soil is considered as known:

$$\tau = 0, \quad t_j(z, 0) = f_j(z). \tag{14.6}$$

The form of function $f_2(z)$ is determined from observation data; $f_3(z)$ is calculated, for instance, by the method outlined in §6.

Kolesnikov /39/ obtained the solution of the problem stated, with conditions (14.2) through (14.4) and (14.6) and with coefficients of turbulent heat exchange in the water and of thermal conductivity below the bottom constant in depth and time. The solution is similar in form to solution (11.1) of the problem of fall cooling of lakes when $\varphi(\tau)=0$ and $\mathbf{Bi}\longrightarrow\infty$. In our notation it assumes the form

$$t_2(z,\tau)=s_2(z)+2\sum_{n=1}^{\infty}\frac{\sin\sigma_n z\cos^2\mu_n h_3 e^{-\nu_n^2\tau}}{h_2\cos\mu_n h_3+\frac{\lambda_2}{\lambda_3}h_3\cos^2\sigma_n h_2}\times$$

$$\times\int_0^{h_2}[f_2(z)-s_2(z)]\sin\sigma_n z\,dz-$$

$$-2\sqrt{\frac{k_2}{k_3}}\sum_{n=1}^{\infty}\frac{\sin\sigma_n z\cos\sigma_n h_2\cos\mu_n h_3 e^{-\nu_n^2\tau}}{h_2\cos\mu_n h_3+\frac{\lambda_2}{\lambda_3}h_3\cos^2\sigma_n h_2}\times$$

$$\times\int_{h_2}^{h_2+h_3}[f_3(z)-s_3(z)]\sin\mu_n(h_2+h_3-z)\,dz, \qquad (14.7)$$

where

$$\sigma_n=\frac{\nu_n}{\sqrt{k_2}},\qquad \mu_n=\frac{\nu_n}{\sqrt{k_3}},$$

$$s_2(z)=\frac{\lambda_3\theta_3 z}{\lambda_3 h_2+\lambda_2 h_3},\qquad s_3(z)=\frac{\lambda_3 h_2+\lambda_2 z}{\lambda_3 h_2+\lambda_2 h_3}.$$

The eigenvalues ν_n are determined by the characteristic equation

$$\mathrm{tg}\frac{\nu}{\sqrt{k_3}}h_3+b\,\mathrm{tg}\frac{\nu}{\sqrt{k_2}}h_2=0, \qquad (14.8)$$

where, as before, $b=\sqrt{\frac{\lambda_3 c_3\rho_3}{\lambda_2 c_2\rho_2}}$.

The first term of expression (14.7) yields the steady temperature distribution in water, determined by the joint action of turbulent exchange in the water and molecular thermal conductivity of the bottom, the lake depth and the propagation depth of annual temperature fluctuations below the bottom, and the mean long-term temperature at this depth below the bottom.

The second term describes the gradually attenuated effect of a deviation from the steady temperature distribution in the water at the initial instant on the further course of the water temperature. The role of this term in the entire process of water temperature variation under the ice is small, and as time passes it rapidly becomes quite insignificant.

The third term describes changes in water temperature owing to heat exchange with the bottom, and this is decisive. The magnitude of this term depends on the entire water–bottom thermal system, especially on the deviation of the initial temperature distribution below the bottom from the steady distribution $s_3(z)$, which characterizes the enthalpy of the bottom at the time of freezing.

Numerical analysis of solution (14.7) showed that for periods exceeding 7 or 8 days (Kolesnikov and Lutkovskii) one may confine oneself to the first four terms of the third sum. This is illustrated in Figure 21, which shows time variations of water temperature at a fixed depth, calculated by the first three (curve 1) and first four (curve 2) terms of the sum. Qualitatively these curves express well the general features of the winter course of water temperature: the winter maximum occurs approximately 50 days after freezing, and the vertical temperature distribution at the time of the maximum is near-steady.

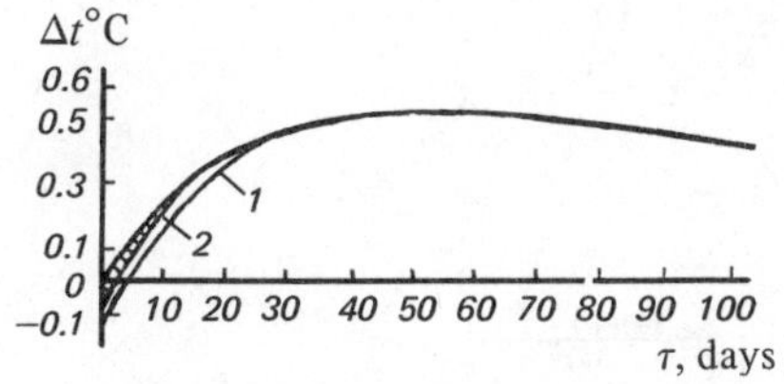

FIGURE 21. Calculation of changes in water temperature under ice using three (1) and four (2) terms of (14.7).

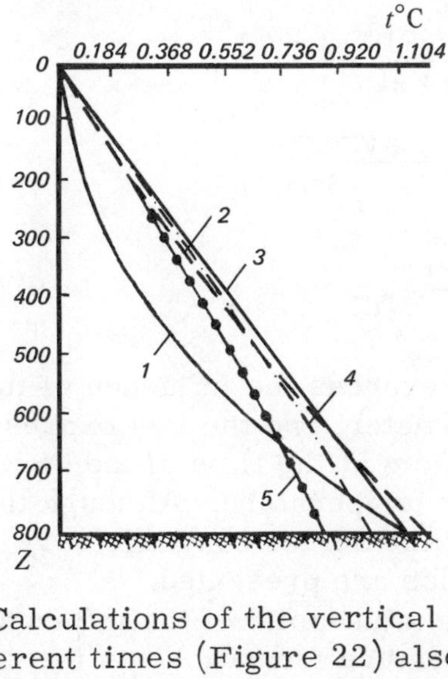

FIGURE 22. Vertical distribution of water temperature under ice cover at different times:

1 — $\tau = 10$ days; 2 — $\tau = 30$ days; 3 — $\tau = 50$ days; 4 — $\tau = 70$ days; 5 — $\tau = 100$ days.

Calculations of the vertical distribution of water temperature at different times (Figure 22) also confirm well the general character (noted in Figure 21) of the course of temperatures for other depths. Before the winter temperature maximum the curves of the temperature distribution with depth are concave ($\tau = 10$ days and $\tau = 30$ days); this indicates that the water is heated at all depths. When the winter maximum is attained, the curves of the vertical temperature distribution become convex, indicating that the entire water–bottom system is cooled.

Thus expression (14.7) describes very correctly the main features of the mechanism governing the formation of winter thermal conditions of water under ice cover, in agreement with observation data. However, the practical application of this method is made complicated by the necessity of preliminarily solving characteristic equation (14.8) to find eigenvalues ν_n. We therefore examine the second solution of equations (14.1), regarding the bottom as a semi-infinite medium /68/. For this we employ Laplace transforms. With conditions (14.2), (14.3), (14.5) and (14.6) we obtain

$$t_2(z,\tau) = \sum_{n=1}^{\infty} \frac{(-1)^n}{2\sqrt{\pi k_2 \tau}} \left(\frac{1-b}{1+b}\right)^n \int_0^{h_2} f_2(\xi) \left[e^{-\frac{(2nh_2 - z + \xi)^2}{4k_2\tau}} - \right.$$

$$\left. - e^{-\frac{(2nh_2 - z - \xi)^2}{4k_2\tau}} \right] d\xi +$$

$$+ \sum_{n=0}^{\infty} \frac{(-1)^n}{2\sqrt{\pi k_2 \tau}} \left(\frac{1-b}{1+b}\right)^n \int_0^{h_2} f_2(\xi) \left[e^{-\frac{(2nh_2 + z - \xi)^2}{4k_2\tau}} - \right.$$

$$\left. - e^{-\frac{(2nh_2 + z + \xi)^2}{4k_2\tau}} \right] d\xi + \frac{b}{1+b} \sum_{n=0}^{\infty} \frac{(-1)^n}{2\sqrt{\pi k_2 \tau}} \left(\frac{1-b}{1+b}\right)^n \times$$

$$\times \int_{h_2}^{\infty} f_3(\xi) \left[e^{-\frac{[(\xi - h_2)\sqrt{k_2} + (2nh_2 + h_2 - z)\sqrt{k_3}]^2}{4k_2k_3\tau}} - \right.$$

$$\left. - e^{-\frac{[(\xi - h_2)\sqrt{k_2} + (2nh_2 + h_2 + z)\sqrt{k_3}]^2}{4k_2k_3\tau}} \right] d\xi. \qquad (14.9)$$

The first two sums of this solution express the influence of the initial temperature distribution in the water, and the last expresses the influence of the enthalpy of the bottom at the time of ice-flow stoppage on the formation of the water temperature. Although the solution obtained seems cumbersome, the series converge very rapidly so that in practice no difficulties are presented.

Consider expression (14.9) from the standpoint of the influence of various factors on the water-temperature formation and the rapidity of series convergence.

The initial temperature distribution at the time of ice-flow stoppage in relatively shallow lakes is sufficiently uniform vertically, and in absolute values the temperatures are close to zero. We therefore approximate function $f_2(\xi)$ by some mean value $\bar{t}_2$ and integrate with respect to ξ the first two sums of (14.9). Designating this part of the solution as $t_2'(z, \tau)$, we obtain

$$t_2'(z, \tau) = \frac{\bar{t}_2}{2} \sum_{n=1}^{\infty} (-1)^n \left(\frac{1-b}{1+b}\right)^n \left\{ \operatorname{erf} \frac{2n+1-x}{2\sqrt{\mathrm{Fo}}} + \right.$$
$$\left. + \operatorname{erf} \frac{2n-1-x}{2\sqrt{\mathrm{Fo}}} - 2 \operatorname{erf} \frac{2n-x}{2\sqrt{\mathrm{Fo}}} \right\} -$$
$$- \frac{\bar{t}_2}{2} \sum_{n=0}^{\infty} (-1)^n \left(\frac{1-b}{1+b}\right)^n \left\{ \operatorname{erf} \frac{2n+1+x}{2\sqrt{\mathrm{Fo}}} + \right.$$
$$\left. + \operatorname{erf} \frac{2n-1+x}{2\sqrt{\mathrm{Fo}}} - 2 \operatorname{erf} \frac{2n+x}{2\sqrt{\mathrm{Fo}}} \right\},$$

where

$$x = z/h_2, \quad \mathrm{Fo} = \frac{k_2 \tau}{h_2^2}. \tag{14.10}$$

Function $t_2'(z, \tau)$ is monotonically damped in time. Using the properties of the error function, it can be shown that when inequality

$$\frac{x}{2\sqrt{\mathrm{Fo}}} \leqslant N \tag{14.11}$$

is satisfied, function t_2' to within some stipulated value N satisfies

$$\frac{t_2'(z, \tau)}{\bar{t}_2} = \operatorname{erf} \frac{x}{2\sqrt{\mathrm{Fo}}} \leqslant N. \tag{14.12}$$

Consequently, with large Fourier numbers satisfying inequality (14.11), the influence of the initial temperature distribution at the time of ice-flow stoppage on the changes in water temperature under the ice may be neglected to within N.

It is easy to estimate the necessary number of terms of the series in (14.10) and of the values of the Fourier numbers that are smaller than in (14.11). For the bottom the estimate is maximal with $x = 1$. Such an estimate, with $(n-1)/\sqrt{\mathrm{Fo}} \geqslant 1$, has the form

$$\left| \frac{t'_{2,n}}{\bar{t}_2} \right| \leqslant \frac{1}{2} \left(\frac{1-b}{1+b}\right)^n \frac{\sqrt{\mathrm{Fo}}}{(n-1)\sqrt{\pi}} e^{-\frac{(n-1)^2}{\mathrm{Fo}}} \leqslant N_1. \tag{14.13}$$

Since the series possess alternating signs and each of their terms decreases in absolute value with increasing number n, n terms yield the approximate value of function $t_2'(z, \tau)$ with an absolute error smaller than the $(n+1)$-th term and with the same sign as that term.

Consider the variation in the last sum in (14.10), expressing the influence of the initial enthalpy of the bottom on the formation of the water temperature. The integrand in each term of this sum is a substantially positive quantity, since $f_3(z)$ is a positive function by the conditions of the problem, and the remainder of the exponent in the square brackets is greater than zero because the exponent of the first of them is smaller than the exponent of the second. Since this is also an alternating series and its terms decrease in absolute magnitude with increasing n, the sum of the entire series is positive. We designate this series $t_2''(z, \tau)$. Since $f_3(z)$ is bounded, it is clear that

$$\lim_{\tau \to 0} t_2'' \to 0 \text{ and } \lim_{\tau \to \infty} t_2'' \to 0.$$

Consequently, function $t_2''(z, \tau)$ has a maximum for all values of the parameters. The absolute value of the maximum and its position in time depend on the thermal characteristics of the water and the bottom, and on the temperature distribution beneath the bottom at the time of ice-flow stoppage.

If the temperature distribution $f_3(z)$ beneath the bottom is approximated by some mean value $\bar{t}_3$, integration with respect to ξ gives

$$t_2''(z, \tau) = \frac{\bar{t}_3}{2} \frac{b}{1+b} \sum_{n=0}^{\infty} (-1)^n \left(\frac{1-b}{1+b}\right)^n \left\{\operatorname{erf} \frac{2n+1+x}{2\sqrt{\mathrm{Fo}}} - \right.$$
$$\left. - \operatorname{erf} \frac{2n+1-x}{1\sqrt{\mathrm{Fo}}} \right\}. \qquad (14.14)$$

The position of the temperature maximum for n terms of the series is in this case

$$\tau_{\max} = \frac{h_2^2}{k_2} \frac{(2n+1)\,x}{\ln \dfrac{2n+1+x}{2n+1-x}}. \qquad (14.15)$$

This expression shows that the time up to the maximum water temperature under the ice is proportional to the square of the lake depth and inversely proportional to the turbulent exchange coefficient in the water. With increasing proximity to the ice cover, and also with each subsequent term of the series, the time of the occurrence of the maximum recedes.

Since in reality the position of the maximum water temperature in time and its absolute value are determined by the sum of $t_2'(z, \tau)$ and $t_2''(z, \tau)$, τ_{max} is also a more complicated function of lake depth and the intensity of turbulent heat exchange in the water. However, expression (14.15) is in good qualitative agreement with observation data, and it shows that in deep lakes with low intensity of turbulent exchange the winter water-temperature maximum occurs later, and it may not even be attained at all during the winter. In the latter case there occurs a gradually attenuated process of continuous increase in water temperature under the ice cover.

On the other hand, in shallow or strongly turbulent lakes the time up to the occurrence of the temperature maximum in winter is short, after which the water begins to cool again. These results are in complete agreement with available observation data on the course of the water temperature of ice-covered lakes.

An assessment of the convergence of the series for t_2'' shows that if the Fourier numbers satisfy the inequality $\sqrt{\mathrm{Fo}}<n$, the maximum value of t_2'' for $z=h_2$ satisfies

$$|t_2''| \leqslant \frac{\bar{t}_3}{2}\frac{b}{1+b}\left(\frac{1-b}{1+b}\right)\frac{n\sqrt{\mathrm{Fo}}}{n\sqrt{\pi}}e^{-\frac{n^2}{\mathrm{Fo}}}. \qquad (14.16)$$

Comparison of (14.13) and (14.16) shows that with the same Fourier numbers for calculating the total variation in water temperature, the series t_2'' requires one term less than the series t_2'. Our computations showed that when $\frac{1-b}{1+b} \leqslant 0.9$, the first three terms of the series in (14.9) yield the course of water temperature throughout winter to within a maximum of 10%.

To illustrate the general variation in different terms in series (14.14) with different Fourier numbers, Figures 23 and 24 show the first two terms and their sum for $x=0.5$ and some values of parameter $\frac{1-b}{1+b}$. It can be seen from Figure 23 that the main features of water-temperature variation as a function of the Fourier number are fully imparted to the first terms of series (14.14). The second term is in the nature of a correction whose role increases with increasing Fourier number. This correction is very small up to the occurrence of the winter temperature maximum.

It may be assumed that the position of the water-temperatur maximum in time and its absolute value can be determined practically by the first terms of the series. Account of the subsequent terms only leads to quicker cooling of the water after the maximum has been attained. The smaller the parameter b, the slower the cooling of the water.

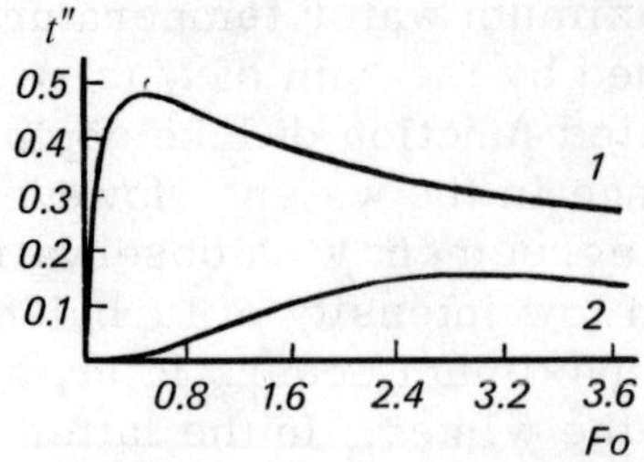

FIGURE 23. Relative value of the first and second terms of the sum (14.14) as a function of the Fourier number.

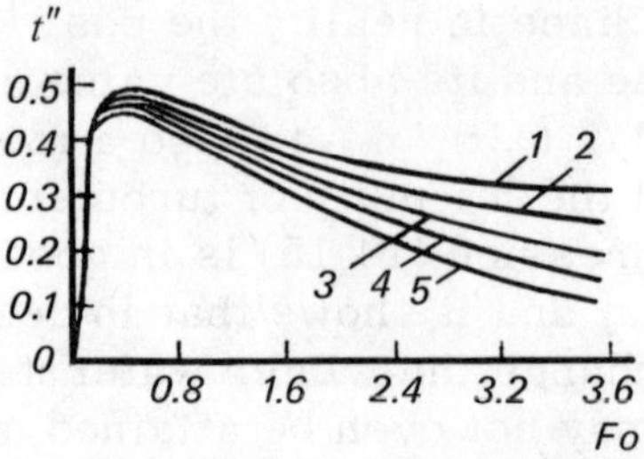

FIGURE 24. Relative value of the sum of the first two terms of (14.14): curves 2—5 correspond respectively to values of parameter $(1-b)/(1+b)$ equal to 0.2; 0.4, 0.6, and 0.8; curve 1 is the algebraic sum of the curves in Figure 23.

The general character of the change in water temperature (Figure 24) is also maintained when the influence of the initial water temperature distribution at the time of ice-flow stoppage is taken into account. If the water temperature at that time is not equal to zero, the rise in temperature after ice-flow stoppage is slower and there is a broader peak.

We give an example of forecasting the water temperature under ice cover in the Ivan'kovo Reservoir. The vertical temperature distribution in the water during ice-flow stoppage is taken as constant, and the calculated bottom distribution is approximated by a step function. Assessments of the thermal characteristics of the water and the bottom of the Ivan'kovo Reservoir /58/ show that we may assume approximately (in CGS units) that $k=4\cdot10^{-2}$, $k_3=2\cdot10^{-2}$, $\lambda_3=8\cdot10^{-3}$. The mean depth of the section in question is $h_2=4$ m.

The calculated course of water temperature at depth $z=0.6\,h_2$ and distance 50 cm from the bottom is compared with observation data in Figure 25. It was found that it suffices to take into account the first two terms of the series, expressing the influence of the initial temperature distribution in the water, and the single first term of the series expressing the influence of the initial enthalpy of the bottom.

Consider the heat-flux time variation in the water under the ice cover with increasing depth. The corresponding general expression can be easily derived by differentiating with respect to z the solutions for the water temperature in the form (14.7) or (14.9), and then multiplying the result by the coefficient of turbulent thermal conductivity of the water:

$$Q_2=-\lambda_2\frac{\partial t_2}{\partial z}. \qquad (14.17)$$

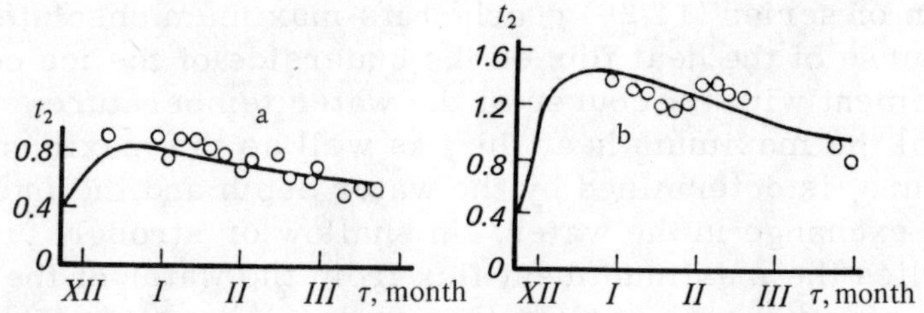

FIGURE 25. Comparison of the calculated (——) and measured (o) course of water temperature at different depths in the Ivan'kovo Reservoir:

a — with $z = 0.6\,h_2$; b — 50 cm from the bottom.

The general analysis of changes in heat flux employs the particular solution in the form of (14.14), i.e., when $f_2(\xi) = 0$. Then, the heat flux from the bottom Q_b is given by

$$Q_b = -\frac{\lambda_2 \bar{t}_3}{2h_2 \sqrt{\pi \mathrm{Fo}}} \frac{b}{1+b} \sum_{n=0}^{\infty} (-1)^n \left(\frac{1-b}{1+b}\right)^n [e^{-\frac{n^2}{\mathrm{Fo}}} - - e^{-\frac{(n+1)^2}{\mathrm{Fo}}}]. \qquad (14.18)$$

In studying this expression we must first point out that the heat flux from the bottom does not change sign, no matter what the Fourier number is, and it is always directed from the bottom into the water. The heat flux attains its maximum value for small Fourier numbers, and it decreases monotonically with increasing Fourier numbers. For any Fourier number **Fo**

$$Q_b \leqslant \frac{\lambda_2 b \bar{t}_3}{4h_2 \sqrt{\pi \mathrm{Fo}}}. \qquad (14.19)$$

Similarly, the heat flux at the water — ice interface is

$$Q_b = -\frac{\lambda_2 \bar{t}_3}{h_2 \sqrt{\pi \mathrm{Fo}}} \frac{b}{1+b} \sum_{n=0}^{\infty} (-1)^n \left(\frac{1-b}{1+b}\right)^n e^{-\frac{(2n+1)^2}{4\mathrm{Fo}}}. \qquad (14.20)$$

Unlike Q_b, quantity Q_i tends to zero as the Fourier numbers tend to zero or infinity. When the Fourier numbers assume the form

$$\mathrm{Fo} = \frac{(2n+1)^2}{2}, \qquad (14.21)$$

each term of series (14.20) reaches its maximum absolute value. Such a course of the heat flux on the underside of the ice cover is in full agreement with the course of the water temperature. The position of the maximum heat flux, as well as the maximum water temperature, is determined by the water depth and the intensity of turbulent exchange in the water. In shallow or strongly turbulent water bodies the maximum heat flux from the water at the underside of the ice cover occurs earlier than in deep or weakly turbulent water bodies.

Numerical calculations (Kolesnikov and Lutkovskii) using the general solution in the form (14.7) lead to the same results. Figure 26 shows the time variation in heat flux to the underside of the ice, and Figure 27 shows the depth variation in heat flux for maximum water temperature ($\tau = 50$ days). Comparison of Figures 21 and 26 indicates that the maximum heat flux occurs somewhat sooner than the maximum water temperature, and the relative changes in heat flux are also smaller than the relative changes in water temperature. The depth distribution of heat flux, as shown in Figure 27, is almost steady, except for a thin water layer at the bottom. This conclusion is very important when finding the rate at which ice builds up or thaws, because it enables us to regard the heat flux from the water to the underside of the ice as constant.

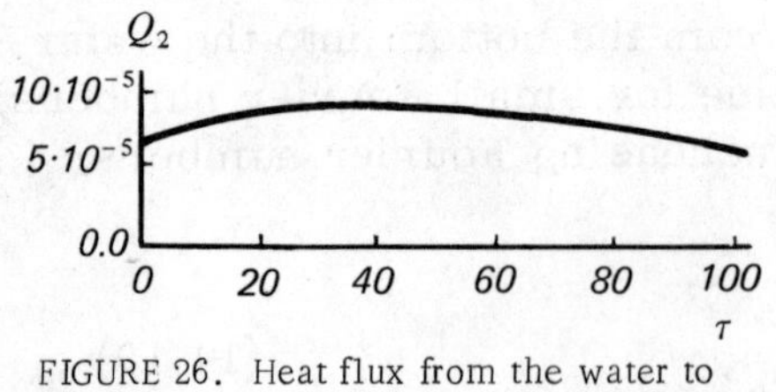

FIGURE 26. Heat flux from the water to the underside of the ice cover as a function of time.

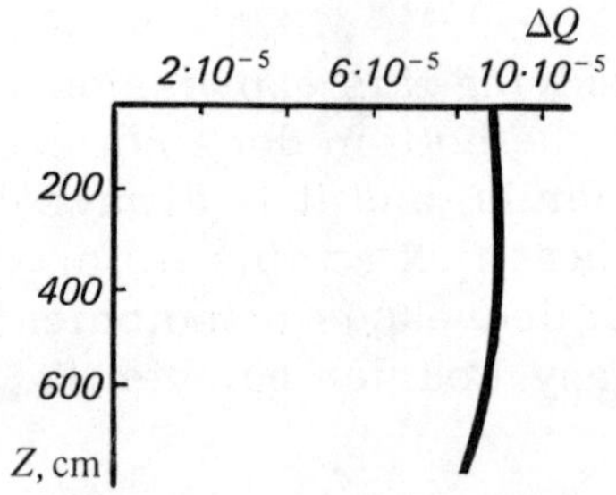

FIGURE 27. Variation in heat flux with lake depth.

Thus the correct theory describes the fundamental laws governing the formation of winter temperature conditions in freezing lakes and rivers and agrees with observation data. The theory can be used to solve problems dealing with buildup or thawing of ice on the underside of ice cover.

§ 15. FORECASTING THE VERTICALLY AVERAGED WATER TEMPERATURE

When solving many practical problems and engineering calculations it is sufficient to have information on the vertically averaged water temperature under the ice. To determine this temperature, the general solutions of (14.7) or (14.9) may be used, if they are integrated over the lake depth. However, the computed relationships in this case are very cumbersome. If the time variability of the thermal and hydrological parameters is also taken into account, the number of computations increases even more.

However, it was pointed out in § 12 that in the fall cooling of lakes the vertically averaged water temperature can be obtained simply and approximately. This solution enables account to be taken of both the influence of the fundamental factors of heat exchange and the change in thermal characteristics and hydrological parameters as a function of length and time. The general form of such a solution is given by expression (12.20), which can be considerably simplified when dealing with forecasting of the vertically averaged water temperature under the ice.

First, in accordance with the accepted schematization of the problem we note that heat exchange with the atmosphere in winter is not among the factors to be determined. The heat flux on the underside of the ice cover can be expressed in the form

$$Q_{\mathrm{i}} = \alpha_{\mathrm{i}} \bar{t}_2,$$

where $\bar{t}_2$ is the vertically averaged water temperature, and α_{i} is the coefficient of heat exchange between water and ice.

This form implies that we must set $\varphi(\tau) = 0$ in the solution of (12.20) for the ice period and replace the total coefficient of heat exchange with the atmosphere α by α_{i}.

Further, if the initial time in the calculation of the vertically averaged water temperature is not taken as the moment of ice-flow stoppage but as the decay of the ice in the previous spring, the initial temperature distribution $f_3(z)$ below the bottom at that time can be replaced by the mean long-term temperature θ_2 of the bottom layers of the water. Then it is easy to calculate the integral with respect to ξ in the last term of (12.21). In view of these considerations the final working formula for forecasting the vertically averaged temperature of ice-covered water of lakes with runoff assumes the form

$$\bar{t}_{2,\nu} = M_\nu' \bar{t}_{2,\nu-1} + \frac{4}{3}\sqrt{\frac{s}{\pi}}\,\frac{\sqrt{\lambda_3 c_3 \rho_3}}{c_2\rho_2 h_2 N_\nu'}\left[\frac{3}{2}(\sqrt{\nu}-\sqrt{\nu-1})\,\theta_2 + \right.$$

$$\left. + \sum_{m=0}^{\nu-1} t_m' \Phi_{m,\nu}\right] + \frac{\bar{q}_{2,\nu} s}{c_2\rho_2 N_\nu'} + \frac{\bar{v}_2 s}{x - x_j}\,\bar{t}_{2,j,\nu}, \qquad (15.1)$$

where M_ν' and N_ν' have the same form as in (12.22) with α replaced by α_i:

$$M_\nu' = \frac{1}{N_\nu'}\left(1 - \frac{\alpha_i s}{c_2\rho_2 h_2} - \frac{\bar{v}_2 s}{x_{j+1} - x_j}\right),$$

$$N_\nu' = 1 + \frac{s}{2}\left(\frac{\alpha_i}{c_2\rho_2 h_2} + \frac{\bar{v}_2}{x_{j+1} - x_j}\right) +$$

$$+ \frac{4}{3}\sqrt{\frac{s}{\pi}}\,\frac{\sqrt{\lambda_3 c_3 \rho_3}}{c_2\rho_2 h_2}\,\mu_3,$$

and function $\Phi_{m,\nu}$ is determined by expression (12.23). Values of the latter function are tabulated in §12. The other notation is as before.

The solution in the form (15.1) is given elsewhere /71/. It determines the vertically averaged water temperature at times $\tau = \nu s$ as a function both of its values at the preceding times, and of the thermal characteristics and hydrological conditions of section j of the lake. Such a form of the solution facilitates forecasting of the water temperature.

We examine the application of formula (15.1) in practical calculations by the example of a lake without runoff /69/. In this case $\bar{v}_2 = 0$ and $\bar{q}_2 = 0$, so that forecasting the water temperature for the entire winter period requires only data on the course of the bottom temperatures in the preceding summer period, the thermal characteristics of the bottom soil, and the coefficient of heat exchange between water and ice.

The course of water temperatures at the bottom in summer may be considered as known. If no such observations exist, it can be approximately stipulated according to the air temperature or calculated from the heat balance of the lake.

The thermal characteristics of the bottom soil enter into the computational relationships only in the form of parameter $\sqrt{\lambda_3 c_3 \rho_3}$. This parameter can be easily determined if there exist simultaneous data on the course of the bottom temperatures of the water and the heat flux from the bottom, for which expression (6.6) suffices.

The greatest difficulty is encountered in selecting the coefficient of heat exchange between water and ice. There are extremely few investigations into this problem. It can be stated with confidence only that the flow rate of the water under the ice has a considerable effect on this coefficient. But to determine the kind of dependence one requires simultaneous heat-flux measurements at the underside of the ice, the vertically averaged water temperature, and the flow rate. If we establish this relationship, it can then be used to select numerical values of the heat exchange coefficient α_i.

When the computational parameters have been stipulated and tables of function $\Phi_{m,\nu}$ are available, the vertically averaged water temperature can be calculated very simply. A row of numbers t_m is set up from the known bottom temperature values for different time intervals s; if $\tau=(\nu-1)s$ corresponds to the time that a continuous ice cover forms on the water surface, then formula (15.1) can be used to determine the temperature at time $\tau=\nu s$. We multiply this temperature by μ_3 and complement the row of numbers denoting bottom temperatures by these values $\mu_3 t_{2\nu}$ and find $t_{2,\nu+1}$ from (15.1). Thus we calculate in successive steps the entire course of the water temperatures under the ice in winter. The thermal and hydrological parameters may change discretely from one period of time to another. Parameter μ_3 may be taken as equal to 2 in approximate calculations.

Figure 28 illustrates the influence of lake depth and variations in the coefficient of heat exchange between water and ice on the course of the vertically averaged temperature (15.1) for lakes without runoff. The resulting solution indicates correctly the general type and the displacement of the water temperature maximum as a function of lake depth and the intensity of turbulent exchange in the water, indirectly characterized by the coefficient of heat exchange between water and ice: an increase in α_i corresponds to increased intensity of turbulent heat exchange in water.

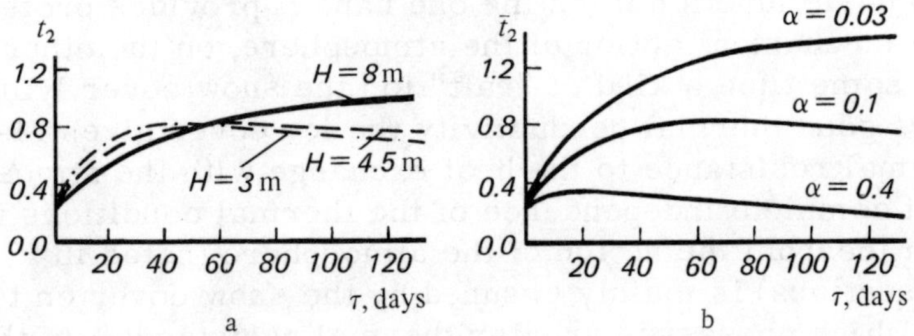

FIGURE 28. Vertically averaged water temperature vs. depth (a) and coefficient of heat exchange between water and ice (b).

Comparison of the calculation results for the vertically averaged water temperature according to (15.1) where $\bar{v}_2=0$ and

$\bar{q}_2 = 0$, with the observation data of the Ivan'kovo Reservoir shows that there is quite satisfactory agreement. Thus this method of forecasting the vertically averaged water temperature under ice is simple to apply practically, yields sufficiently reliable results, and may also be used in engineering calculations when planning the thermal regime of the water of ice-covered lakes and rivers.

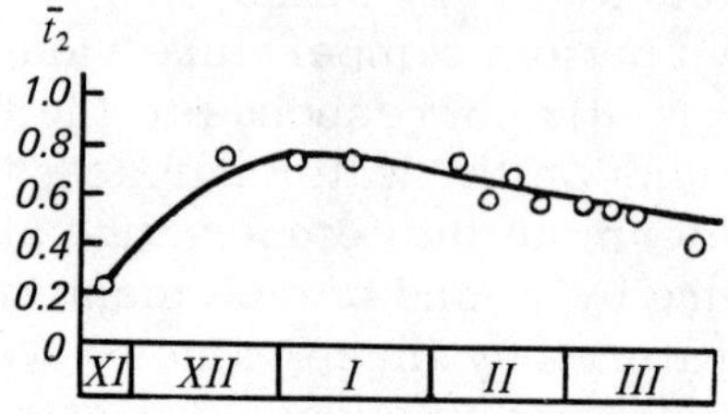

FIGURE 29. Comparison of calculated (———) and measured (o) course of vertically averaged water temperature.

§16. BUILDUP AND THAWING OF ICE COVER

The analytical investigation of the buildup and thawing of ice is a very complicated problem entailing a moving interface separating water and ice. Stefan, Shvets /89/, Kritskii et al. /58/, and Kolesnikov investigated such a problem, and introduced a number of simplifying assumptions. Before explaining their main results we make the following comments.

The ice cover on the surface of lakes and rivers in winter fulfills two basic functions: on the one hand it provides protection against the mechanical action of the atmosphere, on the other hand it is at the same time a kind of "raft" for the snow cover lying on it. Owing to its good thermal conductivity the ice cover gives rise to low thermal resistance to the heat exchange with the atmosphere. The almost complete independence of the thermal conditions in water under ice from the action of the atmosphere (noted in preceding sections) is mainly ensured by the snow cover on top of the ice, which possesses greater thermal resistance. In this connection it is seen that the roles of the ice and snow covers in forming the winter thermal conditions of lakes and rivers differ greatly.

Owing to the low buoyancy of ice (the difference between the specific weights of water and of ice is about 8%) the depth of the snow cover that the ice can support is limited. In the equilibrium state the ratio between the thickness of ice and snow is determined by

$$\frac{h_s}{h_1} = \frac{\rho_2 - \rho_1}{\rho_s}, \tag{16.1}$$

where ρ_2, ρ_1, ρ_s are the densities of water, ice, and snow, respectively; h_1 and h_s are the thickness of the ice and the depth of snow on it.

If, for an estimate (in the CGS system), $\rho_2 = 1$, $\rho_1 = 0.92$, and $\rho_s = 0.2$, then

$$\frac{h_s}{h_1} = 0.4.$$

If there is abundant snowfall, the depth of the snow cover on the ice may exceed the value following from condition (16.1). In that case the limit equilibrium of the ice and snow cover is infringed, and the ice cover becomes overloaded. The stresses induced thereby cause cracks to appear in the ice cover, which is severed from the shores; water then begins to cover the upper surface of the ice so that part of the snow cover with its underside enters the water. Under these conditions the thermal conditions of the ice and snow cover are also rather special. That part of the snow which is saturated with water is a region of zero temperature. Heat exchange with the atmosphere through the dry snow cover causes the water-saturated snow to freeze, and the influx of heat from the water leads to thawing from the underside of the ice. The limit equilibrium in the relation between the thickness of ice and snow is again restored.

The general problem of the buildup or thawing of ice, taking into account the dynamic factors pertaining to the overloading of the ice cover and the formation of snow ice, cannot yet be described strictly and quantitatively. We therefore confine ourselves henceforth to examining ice-formation processes at the water – ice interface (Kolesnikov and Lutkovskii).

The main initial equation in investigating the buildup or thawing of ice on its underside in contact with water is the balance equation of ice formation:

$$\rho_1 \gamma_1 \frac{dh_1}{d\tau} = Q_1 - Q_2, \tag{16.2}$$

where γ_1 is the crystallization temperature of ice, Q_2 is the heat flux from the water, Q_1 is the heat flux through the ice and snow into the atmosphere.

The determination of heat flux Q_2 from the water to the underside of the ice cover was examined in detail in §14. However, if the corresponding general expressions for Q_2 are used, it complicates very much the solution of the problem. Therefore in most investigations one resorts to some schematic course of Q_2 vs. time. For relatively short time intervals (of the order of 10 days) it is usually assumed that the heat flux from the water is constant. This assumption provides a sufficiently accurate picture of reality as regards changes in Q_2 during short intervals of time.

Determination of the heat flux through the ice and snow into the atmosphere involves solving the problem of the temperature regime of the ice — snow system under the condition of total heat balance on the surface of the snow, in order to express the effect of the thermal action of the atmosphere. In the general case of nonsteady thermal conditions such a problem is very complicated, and the solutions obtained are unsuitable for theoretical analysis and practical calculations dealing with the buildup or thawing of ice. Therefore, to determine Q_1, a schematization of actual conditions is also used; it consists in assuming that the thermal conditions in ice and snow covers are quasi-steady.

Within the framework of these assumptions we shall examine the buildup or thawing of ice at its underside. Known initial data comprise the heat flux Q_2 from the water, the flux of total solar radiation I_0, the effective radiation $R_0(\tau)$ of the black surface of the pyrgeometer, air temperature $t_0(\tau)$, water vapor pressure $e_0(\tau)$, and wind speed $v_0(\tau)$ measured at some height h_0 in the air, and also the thermal characteristics of the ice and snow, and of the turbulence in the atmosphere. If these data are available, and if the thermal conditions of the ice, snow, and the surface layer are steady, then the heat flux can be expressed in terms of the main components of the heat exchange with the atmosphere. If we apply the concept of equivalent temperature (cf. e. g., (9.3)), we have

$$Q_1 = \frac{\theta}{\dfrac{h_1 + h_{in}}{\lambda_1} + \dfrac{h_s}{\lambda_s} + \dfrac{1}{\alpha_s}}, \tag{16.3}$$

where

$$\alpha_s = \alpha_0 + 4\delta_s \sigma T_0^3 + \alpha_q l e_1,$$

$$\theta(\tau) = \frac{\alpha_0 + 4\alpha\delta_s T_0^3}{\alpha_s} t_0 + \frac{1 - A_s}{\alpha_s} I_0 - \frac{\delta_s R_0}{\alpha_s} - \frac{\alpha_q l}{\alpha_s}(\bar{e} - e_0),$$

$$\alpha_0 = c_0 \rho_0 \Bigg/ \int_0^{h_0} \frac{dz}{k_0(z)}, \qquad \alpha_a = 0.623 \rho_0 \Bigg/ \mathrm{B}_0 \int_0^{h_0} \frac{dz}{k_0(z)}$$

c_0 and ρ_0 are the specific heat and density of air, A_s is the albedo of snow or ice, λ_l and λ_s are the thermal conductivity coefficients of ice and snow, $k_0(z)$ is the coefficient of turbulent heat exchange in the atmosphere, h_{in} is the initial ice thickness, σ is the Stefan–Boltzmann constant, δ_s is the relative radiating power of snow or ice, $\mathbf{B}_0$ is the barometric pressure, e and e_1 are coefficients in the linear dependence $e_{in}=\overline{e}+e_1 t_s$ of the water vapor pressure e_{in} at the temperature of the snow or ice.

Expression (16.3) can be used to derive the basic balance equation of ice formation (16.1) on the underside of the ice cover:

$$\gamma_1\rho_1\frac{dh_1}{d\tau}=\frac{\theta}{\dfrac{h_1+h_{in}}{\lambda_1}+\dfrac{h_s}{\lambda_s}+\dfrac{1}{\alpha_s}}-Q_2.$$

Integration of this equation with all quantities constant except h_1 yields, over the interval of computation,

$$-\frac{\theta^2\lambda_1}{Q_2^{\,2}}\ln\left(1-\frac{Q_2h_1}{\lambda_1B\theta}\right)-\frac{\theta}{Q_2}h_1=\frac{\theta}{\gamma_1\rho_1}\tau, \tag{16.4}$$

where

$$B=1-\frac{Q_2}{\theta}\left(\frac{h_{in}}{\lambda_1}+\frac{h_s}{\lambda_s}+\frac{1}{\alpha_s}\right).$$

Kritskii /58/ obtained a similar formula and corresponding special nomographs. The main difference is that he determined the components of heat exchange with the atmosphere by empirical formulas.

Expression (16.4) is inconvenient for mathematical analysis and practical calculations, because it is transcendental with respect to h_1. It must therefore be transformed to a more convenient form making use of the fact that $Q_2h_1/\lambda_1B\theta$ is small. Then $(1-Q_2h_1/\lambda_1B\theta)$ can be expanded as a series (Kolesnikov and Lutkovskii).

If we retain only the first two terms of the series, equation (16.4) reduces to a quadratic equation in h_1, with solution

$$\Delta h_1=B\left[\sqrt{\left(h_{in}+\frac{h_s\lambda_1}{\lambda_s}+\frac{\lambda_1}{\alpha_s}\right)^2+\frac{2\lambda_1\theta}{\rho_1\gamma_1}\Delta\tau}-\left(h_{in}+\frac{h_s\lambda_1}{\lambda_s}+\frac{\lambda_1}{\alpha_s}\right)\right]. \tag{16.5}$$

An assessment of such an approximation shows that for some average conditions the error in the buildup of ice from 1 to 10 cm does not exceed 1%. The time interval of such a calculation need not be more than 10 days.

Expression (16.5) facilitates analysis of the effect of different factors on the buildup of ice and the derivation of working formulas corresponding to the different initial data stipulated. Suppose the snow surface temperature is known as initial data. The expression for calculating the buildup of ice in this case is obtained from (16.5), if $\theta = \theta_s$ and $\alpha_s \to \infty$. The result is

$$\Delta h_1' = B' \left[\sqrt{\left(h_{in} + \frac{h_s \lambda_1}{\lambda_s}\right)^2 + 2 \frac{\lambda_1 \theta_s}{\rho_1 \gamma_1} \Delta\tau} - \left(h_{in} + \frac{h_s \lambda_1}{\lambda_s}\right)\right].$$

$$B' = 1 - \frac{Q_2}{\theta_c} \left(\frac{h_{in}}{\lambda_1} + \frac{h_s}{\lambda_s}\right).$$

If there is no snow cover on the ice and the effect of heat flux from the water to the underside of the ice is neglected, an even simpler expression is obtained:

$$\Delta h_1'' = \sqrt{h_{in}^2 + 2 \frac{\lambda_1 \theta_1}{\gamma_1 \rho_1} \Delta\tau}\,.$$

As regards its structure this expression fully coincides with the known solution of Stefan pertaining to the movement of the freezing boundary in a two-phase medium and existing empirical formulas for the buildup of ice /15, 61/.

Proceeding from general expression (16.5), we examine in more detail the effect of hydrological conditions on changes in ice thickness brought about by heat flux from the water to the underside of the ice cover, which is expressed quantitatively by the factor B. With the other factors invariable, an increase in heat flux from the water leads to a reduction in ice thickness. However, as mentioned before, Q_2 is determined by the heat reserve of the bottom soil, the intensity of turbulent exchange in the water, and the dissipation of the flow energy into heat. Turbulent exchange in the water is also mainly determined by the flow rate of the water. Thus the buildup or thawing of ice on its underside is closely connected with the flow conditions in the lake or river.

On the basis of available experimental and theoretical data, Kolesnikov related heat flux Q_2 from the water to the underside of the ice and the flow rate (Figure 30). It can be seen that Q_2 increases rapidly with increasing flow rate, especially for speeds greater than 0.3 or 0.4 m/sec. It follows from this graph and expression (16.5) that the ice is thinner on sections with high speed. Such a distribution of ice thickness and flow rates of water is indeed found in natural conditions. A quantitative assessment of changes in ice thickness as a function of flow rate, other conditions remaining unchanged, can be obtained from (16.5), taking Figure 30 into account.

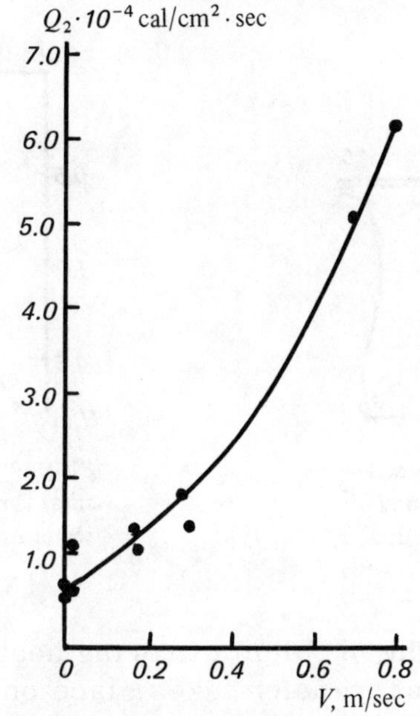

FIGURE 30. Heat flux to the underside of the ice as a function of flow rate.

§17. SPRING HEATING AND DIURNAL COURSE OF THE WATER TEMPERATURE UNDER ICE COVER

As the radiant energy flux increases in spring and the snow cover melts, part of this flux begins to penetrate into the water. The radiant energy penetrating into the water is attenuated least when the snow and snow ice have completely melted, during heating of water by the flux of radiant energy penetrating through the ice cover and being absorbed in the water, and when the vertical water-temperature distribution assumes the characteristic features with the temperature maximum at some distance from the ice cover. As an illustration of radiative heating, Figure 31 shows the vertical distribution of water temperature in different parts of the Klyaz'ma Reservoir /77/. The general vertical temperature distribution in different parts remains the same, but the magnitude and position of the temperature maximum differ somewhat, obviously due to various features in the structure of the ice cover and the hydrological conditions of the different sections.

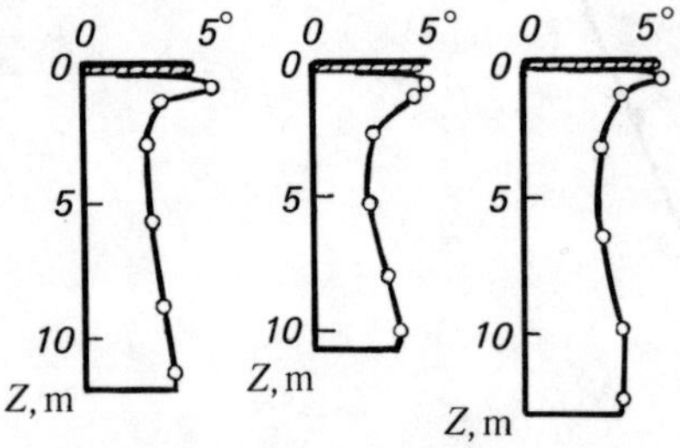

FIGURE 31. Distribution of the water temperature under ice during spring heating of the Klyaz'ma Reservoir.

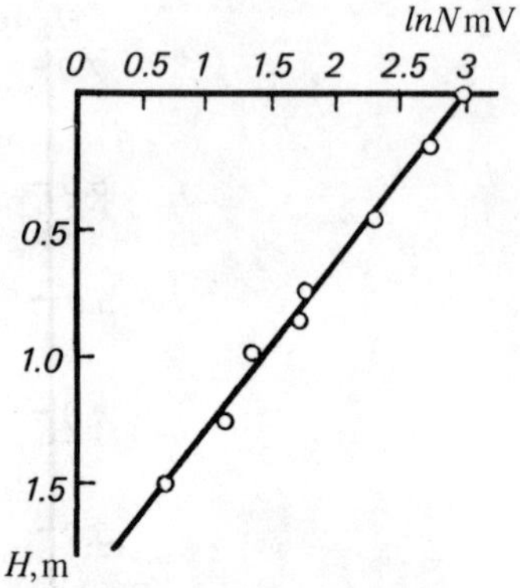

FIGURE 32. Attenuation of the total flux of radiant energy in water under an ice cover.

In the statement of the problem of spring heating of water under ice, we assume that heat transfer takes place only vertically and is effected by turbulent exchange and the flux of radiant energy penetrating through the ice. Since the main zone of heating extends only to a relatively small depth below the ice cover, most lakes and rivers may be considered infinitely deep in solving this problem. Such a statement of the problem expresses actual conditions with sufficient accuracy.

The attenuation of radiant energy in water, and in the snow and ice covers was examined in detail in §2. With allowance for the selectivity of the attenuation, the flux of radiant energy penetrating into these media is in general expressed by formula (2.6), which may be simplified when applied to our problem. When ice is present on the surface of the water, the bulk of the longwave part of the spectrum of radiant energy flux is absorbed by the ice cover. In that case the attenuation of that part of the radiant energy flux passing into the water can be described by the simple exponential function

$$Q(z, \tau) = (1 - A_i) I_0 p e^{-\beta z} = Q_0(\tau) p e^{-\beta z} \qquad (17.1)$$

where I_0 is the radiant energy flux on the upper ice surface, A_i is the ice albedo, β is the coefficient of volume attenuation of radiant energy in the water, and p is a factor which indicates the fraction of I_0 reaching the underside of the ice cover.

The practical use of equation (17.1) under actual conditions is well illustrated by Figure 32, which represents the results of measuring the attenuation of radiant energy flux in the water under an ice cover at the Uchinskoe Reservoir /50/. The coefficient of volume attenuation of radiant energy, found from these measurements, is 1.6 m^{-1}.

The mathematical statement of the problem of spring heating of water under an ice cover, with the accepted assumptions and taking (17.1) into account, reduces to the solution of the heat transfer equation

$$\frac{\partial t_2}{\partial \tau} = k_2 \frac{\partial^2 t_2}{\partial z^2} + \frac{Q_0 p \beta}{c_2 \rho_2} e^{-\beta z} \qquad (17.2)$$

with boundary conditions

$$z = 0, \quad t_2 = 0,$$
$$z \to \infty, \quad t_2 = \text{const} \qquad (17.3)$$

and initial condition

$$\tau = 0, \quad t_2 = f_2(z).$$

The solution of the stated problem can be obtained as a special case of a more general problem examined in § 9. Assuming in (9.11) and (9.8) that $\varphi = 0$ and $\alpha \longrightarrow \infty$, we obtain

$$t_2(z, \tau) = \frac{1}{2\sqrt{\pi k_2 \tau}} \int_0^\infty f_2(\xi) \left[e^{-\frac{(z-\xi)^2}{4k_2\tau}} - e^{-\frac{(z+\xi)^2}{4k_2\tau}}\right] d\xi +$$
$$+ \frac{p\beta}{2c_2\rho_2} \int_0^\tau Q_0(\eta) \{\Phi_\beta(-z, \tau-\eta) - \Phi_\beta(z, \tau-\eta)\}\, d\eta, \qquad (17.4)$$

where

$$\Phi_\beta(z, \tau) = e^{\beta z + \beta^2 k_2 \tau} \operatorname{erfc}\left(\frac{z}{2\sqrt{k_2\tau}} + \beta\sqrt{k_2\tau}\right). \qquad (17.5)$$

If we approximate the time variation of the total flux of radiant energy and the initial temperature distribution in the water by mean values $\overline{Q}_0$ and $\overline{t}_2$, then integration of expression (17.4) yields

$$t_2(z, \tau) = \bar{t}_2 \operatorname{erf} \frac{z}{2\sqrt{k_2\tau}} - \frac{p\bar{Q}_0}{2c_2\rho_2 k_2\beta}\left[\Phi_\beta(z, \tau) - \right.$$
$$\left. -\Phi_\beta(-z, \tau) - 2\operatorname{erfc}\frac{z}{2\sqrt{k_2\tau}} + 2e^{-\beta z}\right]. \qquad (17.5')$$

The first term of (17.4) or (17.5') describes the attenuating effect of the initial temperature distribution in the water. The other terms characterize radiative heating of the water under the ice as a result of the absorption of radiant energy.

It can be easily seen that the obtained solution yields the vertical distribution of water temperature with a maximum at some distance from the ice cover; its position is determined by the transparency of the water and the intensity of the turbulent exchange.

If the initial temperature distribution is neglected, the position of the maximum satisfies the transcendental equation

$$\operatorname{erfc}\left(\frac{z}{2\sqrt{k_2\tau}} + \beta\sqrt{k_2\tau}\right) + e^{-\beta z}\operatorname{erfc}\left(-\frac{z}{2\sqrt{k_2\tau}} + \right.$$
$$\left. + \beta\sqrt{k_2\tau}\right) = 2e^{-2\beta z - \beta^2 k_2\tau}.$$

If we assume for the estimates that the coefficient of turbulent exchange in water $k_2 = 5 \cdot 10^{-3}$ cm^2/sec, the coefficient of volume attenuation of radiant energy in water $\beta = 1.6 \cdot 10^{-2}$ cm^{-1}, and time $\tau = 1$ day, we obtain the position of the maximum; $z_{max} = 40$ cm from the underside of the ice cover. If the intensity of turbulent exchange or the time interval increases and the water transparency decreases, i.e., if parameter $\beta\sqrt{k_2\tau}$ increases, the temperature maximum is situated at greater depth. These results are in good agreement with observation data on radiative heating of water under ice.

Diurnal fluctuations in the radiant energy that penetrates through the ice into the water also induce corresponding changes in water temperature. The depth to which diurnal temperature fluctuations in the water propagate and their amplitude are determined by the transparency of the ice and water and by the intensity of turbulent mixing.

Kolesnikov and Speranskaya /50/ examined diurnal temperature fluctuations of water under ice due to the absorption of the sun's radiant energy. Mathematically the problem amounts to solving equation (17.2) with boundary conditions (17.3), governing temperature deviations from the mean diurnal value. The initial condition is that periodic changes in temperature possess the same period as the variations in radiant energy flux.

The deviations in radiant energy flux penetrating into the water can be expressed in the form of a Fourier series. The solution of the problem is also sought in the form of a Fourier series. Kolesnikov and Speranskaya hence obtained the following expression for the temperature deviations:

$$t_2'(z,\tau) = \sum_{n=1} \frac{p\beta}{c_2\rho_2} \sqrt{\frac{A_n^2 + B_n^2}{(k_2\beta^2)^2 + (n\omega)^2}} \Big\{ \cos\Big(n\omega\tau - \\ - \sqrt{\frac{n\omega}{2k_2}}\, z + \operatorname{arctg} \frac{n\omega A_n - k_2\beta^2 B_n}{k_2\beta^2 A_n + n\omega B_n} \Big) e^{-\sqrt{\frac{n\omega}{2k_2}}z} - \\ - e^{-\beta z} \cos\Big(n\omega\tau + \operatorname{arctg} \frac{n\omega A_n - k_2\beta^2 B_n}{k_2\beta^2 A_n + n\omega B_n} \Big) \Big\}, \qquad (17.6)$$

where A_n and B_n are the coefficients of the Fourier expansion of the deviations of radiant energy flux $Q_0(\tau)$ from its mean diurnal value.

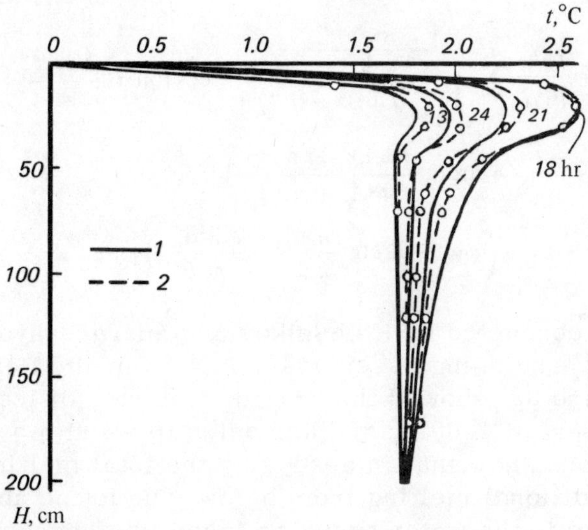

FIGURE 33. Comparison of the temperature distribution under ice at different times, calculated by (17.6) and measured.

The first sum in this solution describes the temperature waves attenuated with depth, the amplitude depending on the radiant energy penetrating through the ice, the transmittance of the water, and the intensity of the turbulent exchange. The second sum also describes a function attenuated with increasing depth and expressing weakening of the radiant energy flux in water. The difference between these two sums yields the temperature distribution in the water, with a maximum at some depth below the underside of the ice.

The calculated temperature distribution is in good agreement with observation data from the Uchinskoe Reservoir (Figure 33).

Diurnal fluctuations of water temperature, determined by the absorption of radiant energy penetrating through the ice into the water, also have a substantial effect on the rate at which ice melts from below in daylight, yielding an additional influx of heat to the underside of the ice cover. In the balance equation of ice formation (16.2) the heat flux in the ice may be neglected during intensive thawing (from the upper and lower ice surfaces), in which case this equation reduces to

$$\gamma_1 \rho_1 \frac{dh_1}{d\tau} = \lambda_2 \frac{\partial t_2}{\partial z}\bigg|_{z=0}.$$

When the water-temperature solution (17.6) is used, the rate of ice melting from below is

$$\frac{dh_1}{d\tau} = \frac{p\beta k_2}{\rho_1 \gamma_1} \sum_{n=1}^{j} \sqrt{\frac{A_n^2 + B_n^2}{(k_2\beta^2)^2 + (n\omega)^2}} \left\{ \cos\left(n\omega\tau + \frac{\pi}{4} + \right.\right.$$
$$\left. + \operatorname{arctg} \frac{n\omega A_n - k_2\beta^2 B_n}{k_2\beta^2 A_n + n\omega B_n} \right)$$
$$\left. - \beta \cos\left(n\omega\tau - \operatorname{arctg} \frac{n\omega A_n - k_2\beta^2 B_n}{k_2\beta^2 A_n + n\omega B_n} \right) \right\} \qquad (17.7)$$

Calculations conducted by Kolesnikov and Speranskaya according to formula (17.7) and using observation data from the Uchinskoe Reservoir (Figure 33) showed that the melting rate of ice from below was greatest at 1500 hr and amounted to about 5.5 mm/hr. These calculations show that in assessing the total melting of ice in spring the additional melting from below, due to the absorption of radiant energy in the water, must be taken into account.

Chapter IV

THE DYNAMICS OF ICE PROCESSES

§18. FORMATION OF SURFACE ICE AND FRAZIL

In examining processes of fall cooling we restricted ourselves to a completely open water surface; the end of this period was regarded as the time when zero temperature was attained at the water surface. Thus the solutions of the problems examined in Chapter II permit one to calculate the time when the first ice forms, but they do not permit one to follow the dynamics of their development up to the formation of a continuous ice cover on the water surface. The analysis of the winter thermal conditions of lakes and rivers did not deal with the dynamics of ice processes on open sections of rivers or lower waters.

The course of these processes is determined by the interaction of a complicated set of hydrometeorological factors, hydrological features of the lake or river, and crystallization of the water during its turbulent mixing. Knowledge of the dynamics of ice processes during ice-flow stoppage is as yet insufficient, and therefore a strictly quantitative statement of this problem cannot yet be given. On the other hand, its solution is extremely important for a number of practical problems, because ice phenomena connected with surface ice and frazil pose the greatest difficulties in hydroelectric power stations and other hydraulic installations.

The first ice formation may occur when zero temperature is attained on the water surface during fall cooling of lakes and rivers. When the cooling continues from the surface, the further dynamics of the ice formation depends essentially on the hydrological conditions of the lake or river in question, chiefly on the intensity of the turbulent exchange in the water.

In lakes with low flow rates and relatively small water surface area the turbulent mixing intensity is low, and the cooling is concentrated in a thin layer close to the surface. If the weather is persistently frosty and the water surface is calm, the water in this layer is soon supercooled and a film of surface ice forms while the total heat reserve of the lake is still positive. The time interval between attaining zero temperature at the water surface and the establishment of a continuous ice cover is short. The ice thickness rapidly increases on account of continued heat exchange with the atmosphere, and the temperature conditions in the water change to the winter phase (cf. Chapter III).

Unstable weather with warm spells and the dynamic action of wind cause the thin surface ice to melt or break, extending the ice-flow stoppage period. If the intensity of turbulent mixing in the water is low, the process of ice formation is in principle unaffected.

An entirely different situation exists in shallow waters with high flow rates and large plane dimensions. Turbulent mixing in such waters extends practically throughout the water down to the bottom. The water temperature is well equalized, and supercooling also extends down to the bottom. Although the supercooling is slight, amounting to between thousandths and tenths of a degree, it is sufficient to cause the water to crystallize over the entire depth of the flow. Thus in waters with intensive turbulent mixing, ice crystals form on the surface as well as under the surface, and this leads to the formation of various kinds of anchor and floating anchor ice, and it also changes the conditions of the formation of surface ice.

The phenomena of frazil and anchor ice, the icing of objects in the water of fast-flowing rivers, and their disastrous consequences have been known for a long time. However, the first investigations of such processes were purely qualitative, describing the natural conditions and stating the facts involved in the occurrence of various types of ice formation. More systematic investigations, entailing also quantitative assessments and laboratory experiments on the crystallization of water, did not begin until the early twentieth century; they were headed by Al'tberg /1/. The most important result of these investigations was to establish that the decisive factors are heat exchange with the atmosphere on the water surface and turbulent mixing. It is precisely these factors which explain how the flow is supercooled, how crystallization under the surface is stimulated in the presence of crystallization nuclei, and how latent heat of crystallization is conducted into the atmosphere.

Further studies into the formation of frazil concentrated on detailing the roles of individual factors from data of observations in nature, depending on the hydrometeorological conditions, and also on laboratory experiments. Without attempting a complete survey, we note that such work under natural conditions was conducted by Vartazarov /16/, Sokolov (1954), Chizhov /88/, Evstifeev /25/, and others. Bibikov /6/, Kumai and Itagaki /102/, Arakawa /93/, Bukina /11, 12, 14/, and others deal with laboratory investigations of frazil.

In fast-flowing mountain streams supercooling may attain 0.1 degree; in the plains it does not exceed 0.02 or 0.03 degree. At the initial stage of crystallization the crystals are small, and these crystals on the whole follow the motion of the water particles in the turbulent flow. If the liberated heat of crystallization is intensively transmitted to the atmosphere and does not reduce supercooling of the water, the crystals that have already formed grow, and new ones form throughout the cross-section of the flow. The increase in crystal size may occur either as a result of the growth of the crystals themselves or by the fusion of small crystals into larger ones. The ice crystals in the water fasten onto various objects on the bottom, and act as a source in the formation of various kinds of anchor ice.

When the ice crystals attain such a size that their hydraulic size exceeds the magnitude of the vertical fluctuation rate in the turbulent flow, they rise to the surface of the water and form slush ice sheets, which are variegated forms of strongly porous ice formations. Anchor ice rises similarly to the surface when its buoyancy exceeds the cohesive force with the bottom.

The numerous observations of frazil formation under natural condition disregard the initial stage of crystallization: the origin of nuclei, their density and growth rate; the distribution of forming and growing crystals according to size and flow section. Generalization of observations in nature is achieved mainly by establishing empirical relations between the integral amount of gruel ice and the hydrometeorological factors. Then stable linear relationships are derived between the thickness of the floating gruel ice and the sum of subzero air temperatures; similar relations are found between the runoff of gruel ice and the sum of subzero air temperatures /22/. Naturally, the coefficients in such relations pertain to different objects or different sections of the same object and do not remain constant; they vary as a function of the hydrological conditions at the place of observation.

The existence of stable relations between the integral amount of gruel ice and the sum of subzero air temperatures can be illustrated physically by the following consideration. The integral quantity of ice which can form in a column of water of unit cross-section when heat exchange with the atmosphere ensures the necessary degree of supercooling and removal of the latent heat of crystallization, is determined by the relation

$$dQ_i = \frac{Q_a}{\rho_1 \gamma_1} d\tau. \qquad (18.1)$$

Since the temperature of the water surface may be assumed to be zero, the heat exchange with the atmosphere Q_a, using the concepts of the total coefficient of heat exchange α and of the equivalent temperature $\theta(\tau)$, is given by

$$Q_a = -\alpha\theta(\tau).$$

On open water surfaces, quantities α and $\theta(\tau)$ for zero temperatures on the water surface assume the form

$$\alpha = \alpha_0 + 4\delta\sigma T_0^3;$$

$$\theta = t_0 - \delta R_0/\alpha + Q_0/\alpha - \frac{\alpha_q l}{\alpha}(e - e_0),$$

where α_0 and α_q are determined in accordance with (9.4).

If this expression is substituted in (18.1) and we then integrate,

$$Q_i = -\int_0^\tau at_0(\tau) - F, \qquad (18.2)$$

where

$$F = \int_0^\tau \{Q_0(\tau) - \delta R_0(\tau) - \alpha_q l\,[e - e_0(\tau)]\}\,d\tau.$$

The first term of this expression describes the effect of turbulent heat exchange with the atmosphere and partly of the effective radiation on the growth of ice crystals in the water, and is proportional to the sum of subzero air temperatures t_0. The second term describes the effect of the other heat exchange components on the water surface, in particular absorption of radiant energy, effective radiation, and evaporation. It may be regarded as the free term in the linear relation between the amount of frazil ice formed and the sum of subzero air temperatures.

Relationship (18.2) could serve for a quantitative assessment of the frazil or gruel ice formed, using the known balance on the water surface. The main difficulty in its application is that coefficients α_0 and α_q cannot be calculated theoretically when there is gruel ice formation on the water surface, because then these coefficients are determined not only by the characteristics of turbulent exchange in the marine surface layer but also by the distribution of slush ice sheets on the surface of the lake or river.

We now examine the main conclusions from laboratory investigations of water crystallization during turbulent mixing. Al'tberg's first experimental investigations established /1/ that the crystals forming in water under laboratory and natural conditions are identical in the initial stage of their formation. With increasing mixing the crystallization process begins at lower supercooling temperatures and takes place very rapidly. Figure 34 shows a typical curve of the course of the water temperature during crystallization, and this permits a quantitative description of the crystallization process.

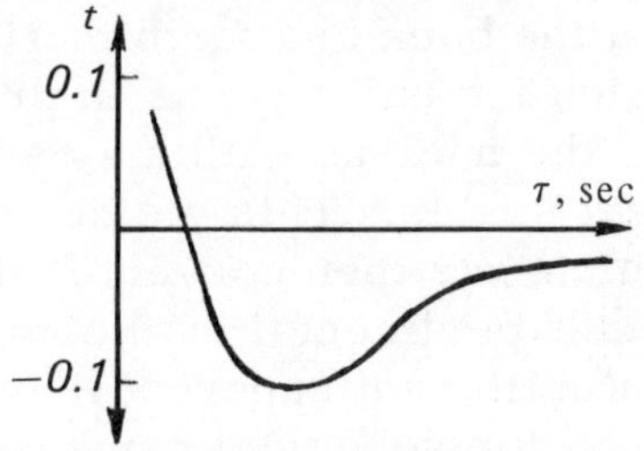

FIGURE 34. Typical time-variation of water temperature during the formation and growth of frazil.

As a result of heat transfer to the air the water in the crystallization vessel becomes colder and reaches some degree of supercooling; the extent of the supercooling varies and depends on the state of the water and on external factors. Sometimes crystallization nuclei may form spontaneously in supercooled water or arrive from outside, giving rise to the formation of frazil. The ice crystals thus forming grow by themselves and induce the appearance of new nuclei, thus turning the crystallization in the water into some kind of chain process.

At the initial stage the liberated heat of crystallization is conducted from the water by heat transfer from the surface, and the water temperature continues to drop, but more slowly than before the onset of crystallization. The amount of heat liberated in the water also increases with increasingly intensive crystallization, and at some time it becomes equal to the heat transfer from the surface. At that instant the water temperature ceases to drop.

When the intensity of crystallization increases further, the amount of liberated heat becomes larger than the heat transfer from the surface, and the water temperature begins to rise; this has a delaying effect on the formation and growth of frazil. The crystallization process begins to be attenuated and the water temperature approaches zero asymptotically.

The shape of the forming ice crystals depends mostly on the degree of water supercooling. If the supercooling is slight (from 0 to -0.3°), disk-shaped crystals predominate. With increasing supercooling the crystals assume more complicated star- or fern-like shapes. Mixing of the water has a substantial effect on the growth rate of the crystals, but only a very slight effect on their shape.

Bibikov /4/ was the first to quantitatively investigate the growth rate of ice crystals in flowing water under laboratory conditions. His experiments involved the back and forth motion of nuclei in supercooled water on which ice buildup was in progress. The amount of ice growing on the nucleus within a certain time was determined with analytical scales. This yielded the volumetric growth rate of the ice which was then converted to the linear growth rate. By generalizing the experimental data obtained for different speeds of the crystals and different supercooling temperatures of the water, Bibikov obtained for spherical crystals the following relationship for the linear growth rate of crystals:

$$\frac{dr}{d\tau} = 0.23\,(2.7\,v^{0.47} + 0.32)\,\frac{(-t)}{\sqrt{r}} \qquad (18.3)$$

where v is the speed of the crystals relative to the water, is the radius of the crystal, t is the temperature of supercooling.

All the heat emerging from the water is used to increase the volume of the ice particles in the water. Thus the equation of the balance of ice formation for particles of spherical shape at the water – ice interface yields

$$\frac{dr}{d\tau} = \frac{\alpha_i\,(-t)}{\rho_1 \gamma_1}, \qquad (18.4)$$

where α_i is the coefficient of heat exchange between water and ice.

Comparison of expressions (18.4) and (18.3) shows that the factor before $(-t)$ in the right-hand part of (18.3) has the physical meaning of coefficient of heat exchange between the water and ice particles of spherical shape. Its explicit form is

$$\alpha_i = \frac{\rho_1 \gamma_1}{\sqrt{r}}\,[0.23\,(2.7\,v^{0.47} + 0.32)]. \qquad (18.5)$$

Bukina /12 – 14a/ carried out a long series of laboratory investigations into the origin and growth of ice crystals in water. A special experimental device permitted microscopic films of crystals up to sizes of 0.01 mm to be obtained as supercooled water flowed round them, and also permitted the water temperature to be recorded continually.

The generalization of experimental data on growth rate, as a function of the diameter of disk-shaped crystals showed that, in addition to the temperature of supercooling and the flow rate of the water, the presence or absence of other crystals in the vicinity of the growing crystals is of substantial importance. If a growing crystal is in the midst of a mass of other crystals, its growth is practically terminated; if it is freely washed by water, it grows uniformly. The linear growth rate as dependent on the temperature of supercooling and the flow rate of the water is expressed empirically in the form

$$\frac{dD}{d\tau} = (1.8 + 0.18\,v)10^{-2}\,(-t). \qquad (18.6)$$

Unlike (18.3), the linear growth rate of disk-shaped crystals according to (18.6) does not depend on the size of the growing crystal.

Bukina's investigation of the temperature dependence of the ratio $\delta = \frac{h}{D}$ and the thickness h to the diameter D of disk-shaped ice crystals in water showed that the value of δ drops substantially with increasing supercooling temperature of the water. Over the investigated water temperature interval,

$$\delta = 0.21\,e^{-12t}.$$

For a smaller temperature interval this relationship can be replaced by a linear one:

$$\delta = 0.20 - 1.45\,t. \qquad (18.7)$$

These same experimental data do not reveal any clear relationship between δ and the flow rate of the water.

Bukina /14a/ used high-speed filming to study the size distribution of ice crystals in water at different stages of crystallization. It was found that when the supercooling temperature attained a maximum, the size distribution of the crystals was qualitatively the same, where

$$h(D) = \frac{b_1^4}{6} D^3 e^{-Db_1},$$

b_1 being an empirical coefficient characterizing the position of the maximum on the size-distribution curve of the crystals.

Coefficient b_1 in different experiments lay between 12 mm^{-1} and 17.7 mm^{-1}, with mean value 14.1 mm^{-1}.

The above results were derived for a stable rate of cooling and flow of the water, stable supercooling temperature, and stable seeding of the water. Changes in the number of crystallization nuclei introduced into the water have a substantial effect on the crystallization process: the larger the number of nuclei, the more intensive is the crystallization.

§19. CRYSTALLIZATION OF WATER DURING TURBULENT MIXING

The latter brief survey of investigations concerned with the formation and growth of ice crystals in turbulent water flow shows how complicated these processes are and how insufficiently they have been studied, under both natural and laboratory conditions. This makes it difficult to work out analytical calculation methods and even to state strictly analytically the problem of water crystallization during turbulent mixing. There are therefore very few theoretical studies along these lines.

Makkaveev /62/ was one of the first to attempt an approximate calculation of the vertical distribution of slush ice in a uniform flow, without taking into account the formation and growth of ice crystals in the water. Assuming a steady-state process, viewing the particles of slush ice as a passive admixture and using the semi-empirical equation of diffusion, Makkaveev derived an exponential expression for the vertical distribution of slush ice concentrations:

$$h = h_0 e^{-\int_0^z (w\rho_{sl}/kg)dz}, \qquad (19.1)$$

where w is the hydraulic size of the slush ice, g the acceleration of gravity, ρ_{sl} the density of the slush ice, k the coefficient of turbulent exchange, and h_0 the concentration of slush ice on the surface.

Knowing the parameters contained in (19.1) and the distribution of the horizontal velocity over the flow section, we can also calculate the total discharge of slush ice. However, such a statement of the problem completely ignores the dynamics of the formation and growth of frazil.

Bibikov's work /5/ aims at determining the number of ice crystals in the water as a function of the supercooling temperature and the flow rate of the water. By analyzing his experimental data (cf. §18) he approximates the variation in water temperature during the crystallization process by the expression

$$t = t_0 e^{-(a\tau)^2},$$

where t_0 is the initial supercooling temperature and a is an empirical coefficient. Using this approximation and the empirical relation for the volumetric growth rate of spherical ice particles, the number of particles n_i of the i-th fraction per unit volume of water for time interval j is governed by

$$h_j = \frac{\frac{c\rho}{\rho_1\gamma_1}(-t_0)\left[1-e^{-(a\tau)^2}\right]}{\{p_1[\operatorname{erf}(a\tau_j)-\operatorname{erf}(a\tau_{j-1})]+\sqrt{V_0}\}^2} - \frac{-\sum_{i=1}^{j-1} n_i\{p_1[\operatorname{erf}(a\tau_j)-\operatorname{erf}(a\tau_{j-1})]-\sqrt{V_0}\}^2}{\{p_1[\operatorname{erf}(a\tau_j)-\operatorname{erf}(a\tau_{j-1})]+\sqrt{V_0}\}^2}, \tag{19.2}$$

where

$$p_1 = \frac{\sqrt{\pi}}{4a}\,1.41\,(2.7\,v^{0.47}+0.32)\,(-t);$$

$$n_i = \frac{c\rho/\gamma_1\rho_1\,(-t_0)\left[1-e^{-(a\tau)^2}\right]}{\left[p_1\operatorname{erf}(a\tau_1)+\sqrt{V_0}\right]^2},$$

V_0 is the volume of ice particles at the initial time.

Bibikov processed the special experiments and computed the number of particles by (19.2). He found that at different supercooling temperatures the number of particles per unit volume of water did not change much, the average number being 1,880 particles per dm^3.*

The most complete statement of the problem dealing with the initial crystallization stage of supercooled water during turbulent mixing was given by Kolesnikov and Belyaeva /44/. They obtained a closed system of equations describing the formation and growth of ice crystals in water until their hydraulic size is smaller than the vertical speed fluctuations, i. e., until the crystals ascend in the water. The main thesis of this theory is now examined briefly.

In deriving the basic equations it is assumed that the supercooling of water at which the first crystals appear is previously known and is small, amounting to 0.01 – 0.1 degree. The crystals are assumed to be disk-shaped with a constant thickness-to-radius

* [The original Russian text erroneously gave this unit as the cube of a decicentner.]

ratio. The crystallization process is thought to be spatially uniform and variable only with time, and the turbulence affecting the crystals to be locally isotropic.

The equation governing time variations in the number of crystals is

$$\frac{dn}{d\tau} = \chi t, \tag{19.3}$$

where χ is the parameter characterizing the change in the rate of appearance of visible crystals during a one-degree change in temperature. This equation disregards the effect of a possible change in the number of crystals due to the fusion of small crystals with large ones by molecular-kinetic or hydrodynamic capture, because available experimental data do not as yet provide a basis for obtaining a clear notion of these processes. Therefore (19.3) refers only to the change in the number of visible large crystals that are not subject to capture.

The equation of the growth of disk-shaped crystals with constant thickness (h)-to-radius (r) ratio $\delta = \frac{h}{r}$ has the form

$$\frac{3}{2}\rho_1\gamma_1 \frac{\delta}{1+\delta}\frac{dr}{d\tau} = \alpha_* t. \tag{19.4}$$

It is assumed that growth occurs both by direct growth of the crystal edges and by the fusion of small crystals. Therefore quantity α_* may be considered as some effective coefficient of heat exchange of the crystal with the water, taking into account heat transfer of the crystal under conditions of turbulent mixing, and the fusion of small crystals:

$$\alpha_* = \alpha_i + \alpha' n' \frac{s'}{s}\Delta\tau, \tag{19.5}$$

where α_i is the coefficient of turbulent heat transfer of the growing crystal, n' is the number of small crystals fusing with large crystals per unit time, α' and s' are respectively the coefficient of heat transfer and the surface area of the small crystal, $\Delta\tau$ is the mean lifetime of a small crystal, s is the surface area of a large crystal.

Available experimental data do not yet enable us to construct a rigorous equation for determining the effective coefficient α_*, because the exact mechanism of crystal growth is unknown, in particular the intensity of fusion of small with large crystals.

Therefore α_* must be expressed by an empirical relationship of the form

$$\alpha_* = f(u, r), \tag{19.6}$$

where u is the relative speed of crystal motion in the water.

Since the equations for determining α_* are not very accurate, we confine ourselves to approximate equations when determining u. Assuming that the change in crystal volume occurs much more slowly than changes in u, the equation governing the latter quantity is

$$\rho_1 \delta \pi r^3 \frac{du}{d\tau} = (\rho_2 - \rho_1)\, \delta \pi r^3 \frac{dv_2}{d\tau} - \eta_2 \rho_2 r^2 u^2, \tag{19.7}$$

where v_2 is the speed of the water flow and η_2 is the shape factor in the quadratic drag law for the crystal motion.

In the region where the crystal is affected, the turbulence is assumed to be locally isotropic. Then equation (19.7) is considerably simplified and reduces to

$$u \simeq m r^{1/3}, \tag{19.8}$$

where m is a parameter depending on the coefficients in (19.7).

This system is closed by the heat balance equation for the entire volume of cooled water in which crystallization occurs:

$$c_2 \rho_2 V_2 (t_0 - t) + \int_0^{\tau} q_2(\tau')\, d\tau' = \int_0^{\tau} \frac{dn}{d\tau'}\, d\tau' \int_{\tau^1}^{\tau} \alpha_* s \cdot t\, d\tau'', \tag{19.9}$$

where $q_2(\tau')$ is the heat transfer on the boundaries of the examined volume.

Thus the system of five equations (19.3), (19.4), (19.5), (19.8), and (19.9) enables one to find all the main characteristics n, t, α_*, u, r of the crystallization process from data on the initial cooling temperature, turbulent mixing, and heat exchange on the boundaries of the cooled water.

Kolesnikov and Belyaeva /44/ examined the solution of this system as applied to Bibikov's experimental conditions, using his empirical relationship (18.5) for α_i and assuming that there was no external heat exchange. The time variation in water temperature is obtained in the form

$$\left(\frac{\chi B_1}{6}\right)^{\frac{1}{3}}\tau = \frac{1}{6y_0^2}\ln\frac{y_0^2 + y_0 y + y^2}{(y_0 - y)^2} +$$

$$+\frac{1}{\sqrt{3y_0}}\operatorname{arctg}\frac{2y + y_0}{\sqrt{3y_0}} - \frac{0.52}{\sqrt{3y_0^2}}, \qquad (19.10)$$

where

$$y_0 = \sqrt[3]{t_0},\quad y = \sqrt[3]{t_0 - t}$$

Expression (19.10) yields a family of curves t that depends on parameter χ. When $\chi = 0.54$ the curve of t coincides well with experimental data (Figure 35).

The number of crystals in the investigated volume is

$$n = n_0 + \chi \int_0^\tau t(\tau')\,d\tau'.$$

Quantity $n - n_0$ as a function of time is plotted in Figure 36.

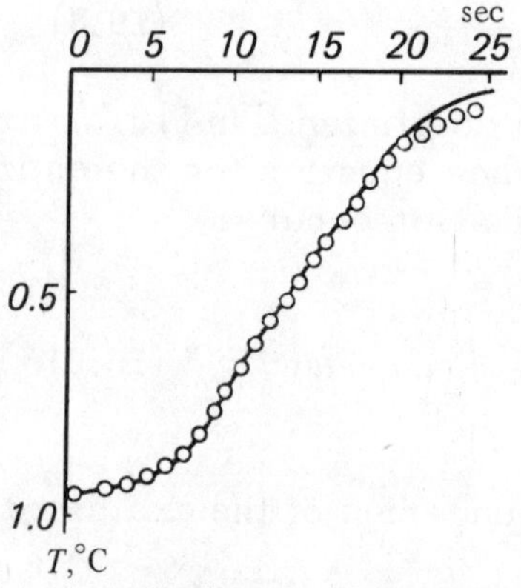

FIGURE 35. Calculated (——) and measured (o) course of water temperature during water crystallization.

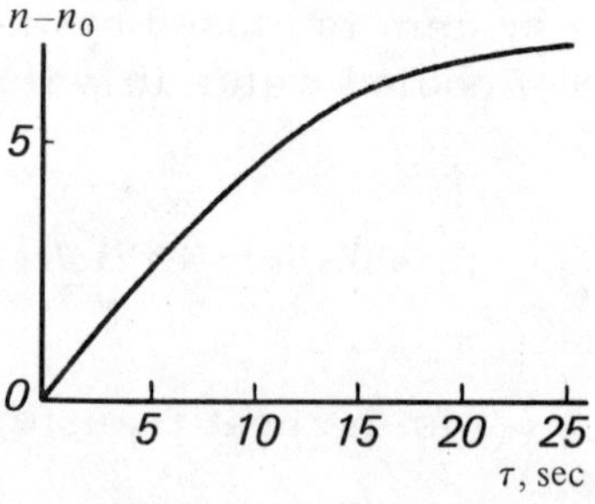

FIGURE 36. Theoretical dependence of the number of crystals on time.

The above theory describes correctly the main features of water crystallization in a turbulent flow. Further investigations under laboratory and natural conditions are required to develop this theory and to refine the initial equations.

§20. THE DYNAMICS OF ICE PHENOMENA ON OPEN SECTIONS OF WATER

It is known that the headwaters of rivers flowing from large lakes and sections of the lower waters emerging from storage lakes are not covered by ice at all during the entire winter. The length of such sections that do not freeze is determined by their hydrological conditions, meteorological conditions, and the sub-ice temperature regime of the lake or storage lake. Depending on these factors the length of the nonfreezing sections may vary from zero to some tens of kilometers in the case of the lower waters of shallow storage lakes /58/.

Throughout winter water with above-zero temperature is discharged into tailraces or rivers. The higher the water temperature beneath the ice in a lake or storage lake and the greater the discharge of water, the greater is the quantity of heat entering the tailrace or river with the water masses. In addition, the water flow regime also changes substantially, being characterized by the transition from low flow rates in the storage lake to high flow rates in the tailrace. Consequently more heat is liberated by the dissipation of flow energy. If the total heat supplied from within the water to the surface exceeds the heat transferred to the atmosphere, an ice cover cannot form.

Moving downstream, the water masses are gradually cooled (by heat exchange with the atmosphere), and at some distance from the discharge the water temperature on the surface reaches zero. Further movement of the water downstream, combined with intensive turbulent mixing, leads to a certain supercooling of the water and to the formation of ice crystals and slush ice. The slush ice that floats up to the surface forms the bulk of ice in the fall and winter debacle on turbulent sections of rivers.

The gradual freezing over and the presence of sheets of slush ice reduce the heat transfer to the atmosphere and turbulent mixing in the water, after which a continuous ice cover forms. The distance between the position of the profile of zero temperatures and the position of the edge of the continuous ice cover is determined by the conditions of heat transfer to the atmosphere and by turbulent mixing in the water. Since actual lakes and rivers are not uniformly deep, water cooling and the formation of a continuous ice cover occur earlier on shallower and calmer sections, so that the zero isotherm and the profile of the edge of the continuous ice cover are curved convex downward in the direction of flow.

The formation of a continuous ice cover in the lower reaches of a river substantially changes the hydraulic and thermal conditions in the adjacent open section. This leads to ice jams causing winter floods and a number of difficulties associated with ice in the work of hydroengineering installations upstream of this section. The edge of the ice which forms raises the water level and reduces the flow rate in the open section. The slush ice coming downstream is partly forced under the ice, but on the whole it accumulates in front of the ice edge. The sheet of slush ice next to the edge is packed increasingly tightly, due to the constant dynamic action of the flow and the pressure of the masses of slush ice upstream. Hence part of the still unfrozen slush ice is forced under the ice cover and thus reduces the clear opening and the throughput capacity of the flow. As a result the edge builds up and the continuous ice cover moves upstream.

If the throughput capacity of the flow is insufficient to let through the slush ice that was forced under the ice, the water level is raised and the sheet of slush ice in front of the edge rises. This creates favorable conditions for the further accumulation of ice material in front of the edge and its packing. The result of repeated packing is an ice jam, which abruptly reduces the throughput capacity of the flow because the river profile becomes clogged by packed slush ice. Therefore the water upstream of the ice jam rises abruptly, with possible flooding of the lower sections of the floodplain /22/.

Unstable meteorological and hydrological conditions along the river and in time greatly increase the unsettled character in the movement of the ice edge. In such a case the analytical description of the dynamics of ice processes in open sections of lakes and rivers is made much more difficult. If the problem is to be stated rigorously, it can be posed only when determining the profile of zero temperatures.

For sections over which the depths are transversally uniform, the problem is similar to that of the fall cooling of storage lakes with runoff (§12). Expression (12.17) or (12.20) with $t_2 = 0$ permits direct determination of the zero temperatures as a function of the water temperature at the discharge, the main components of the heat exchange with the atmosphere, and of the liberation of heat by dissipation of flow energy. The problem of computing the thermal conditions in the section between the profile of zero temperatures and the edge of the continuous ice cover and its shift cannot be stated with sufficient rigorousness; only integrating methods using data from nature can be used here.

Kritskii, Menkel', and Rossinskii /58/ proposed an approximate method of calculating the movements of the ice edge in the lower water by resorting to the following schematization.

The position of the ice edge at any instant of time tends toward the position of stabilization of the profile, which is in close proximity to the profile of zero temperatures. The position of the ice edge undergoes complicated fluctuating motions as a result of changes in meteorological and hydrological conditions, and after a long time coincides on the average with the profile of stabilization. The speed with which the ice edge moves upstream is determined by the ice thickness at the edge and by the quantity of ice carried by the current. The speed of recession is also determined by the ice thickness at the edge and by the amount of heat supplied to it from the water.

The movement of the ice edge is calculated by the heat balance equation for the section that does not freeze. The main heat sources comprise heat arriving with the water from the lake or storage lake, and heat influx from the bottom and dissipation of flow energy into heat. Heat expenditure is effected by heat exchange with the atmosphere through the open water or ice surface. Under these conditions the method of calculating ice-edge movement has two stages: determining the position of the profile of zero temperatures and determining the amount of ice material forming in the section between the profile of zero temperatures and the profile of ice-edge stabilization.

The integral heat balance equation for the section of the open water surface of length L, under steady-state conditions yields

$$T_2 = T_{\text{н}} - \frac{Q_a - Q_2}{c_2\rho_2 q_2} L, \qquad (20.1)$$

where T_2 is the vertically averaged water temperature in the section L, $T_{\text{н}}$ is the vertically averaged water temperature at the discharge of the investigated section, q_2 is the discharge of water per unit cross-section $q_2 = v_2 h_2$, v_2 is the mean velocity, h_2 is the current depth, Q_a is the heat exchange with the atmosphere, $Q_2 = Q_b + Q_d$, Q_b is the heat flux from the bottom, Q_d is the amount of heat liberated by dissipation of flow energy.

The heat balance equation for the lake or river surface is

$$\alpha (T_2 - t_2) = Q_a, \qquad (20.2)$$

where α is the coefficient of heat exchange in the water and t_2 is the temperature at the water surface.

For the position of the profile of zero temperatures, $t_2 = 0$. Then (20.1), taking into account (20.2) with $t_2 = 0$, provides the position of the profile of zero temperatures or of the profile of the onset of ice formation:

$$L_i = \frac{c_2\rho_2 q_2 (T_{\text{н}} - Q_a/\alpha_0)}{Q_a - Q_2}.$$

If temperature T_{H} is slightly above zero and heat transfer from the water surface is intensive, L_{i} may be negative. This means that the process of ice formation begins directly at the source of the river or the discharge into the tailrace.

If we extend expression (20.2), with $t_2 = 0$, to the section between the profile of zero temperatures and the position of the ice edge when this position is stable, we obtain some fictitious temperature at the ice edge,

$$T_{\text{e}} = Q_{\text{a}}/\alpha_{\text{e}} \ ,$$

and the corresponding position of the stabilization profile:

$$L_0 = \frac{c_2 \rho_2 q_2 (T_{\text{H}} - Q_{\text{a}}/\alpha_{\text{e}})}{Q_{\text{a}} - Q_2} \ .$$

It is assumed in investigations into the movements of the ice edge that the position of the stabilization profile coincides with that of the profile of zero temperatures, and that the section of the ice cover within the limits of each time interval corresponds to the shapes established for the mean speed of the edge motion. For these conditions the equation governing the motion of the ice edge is expressed in the form

$$\frac{dL_{\text{e}}}{d\tau} = - A_0 (Q_{\text{a}} - Q_2)(L_{\text{e}} - L_0),$$

where $A_0 = \dfrac{1}{\gamma_1 h_{\text{i}}}$; $h_{\text{i}} = h_{\text{H}}$, the initial thickness of the ice at the edge during its formation ($L_{\text{e}} > L_0$); $h_{\text{i}} = h_{\text{a}}$, the actual thickness of the ice on the river or in the lower water when the ice edge melts ($L_{\text{e}} < L_0$).

If the parameters in the latter equation are constant, integration yields

$$L_{\text{e}} = L_{\text{in}} + (L_{\text{in}} - L_0)(e^{-A_0(Q_{\text{a}} - Q_2)\Delta\tau} - 1). \qquad (20.3)$$

This expression allows one to calculate the change in the position of the ice edge after various time intervals from its known initial value, and the main meteorological and hydrological elements that determine heat transfer to the atmosphere and the liberation of heat in the water.

The greatest difficulties in the practical application of (20.3) are encountered in fixing the numerical values, or dependences on the hydrological regime, of the heat exchange coefficient in the water and of the initial ice thickness. So far no data have been obtained by direct experimental determination of these values. Kritskii et al. /58/ recommend the following relationships for approximate estimates:

$$\alpha_0 = 0.01\, v_2 \quad \text{kcal/m}^2 \cdot \text{day} \cdot \text{deg};$$

$$\alpha_e = 0.002\, v_2 \quad \text{kcal/m}^2 \cdot \text{day} \cdot \text{deg};$$

$$h_н = 0.5\, v_2.$$

These relationships were obtained by analyzing empirical material and express the effect of one of the main factors, the flow rate of the water.

The quantity of heat originating by the dissipation of flow energy is

$$Q_d = \frac{\rho_2 q_2 I}{427},$$

where I is the gradient of the flow. Heat exchange with the bottom soil can be calculated by the methods described in §6. For mean conditions this flux is about 0.1 kcal/m^2· day.

When determining heat exchange with the atmosphere, the authors recommend empirical relationships obtained by generalizing observation material and relating the value of Q_a with the main actinometric and meteorological elements. An opportunity also arises here to use the more general methods examined in Chapter I, with a correction for the presence of ice on the water surface.

It has not yet proved possible to calculate theoretically the initial position of the ice edge at the time of ice-flow stoppage in fall; it must be determined from data of observations in nature.

Comparison of calculated results concerning the movement of the ice edge with observation data showed that there is satisfactory agreement. This indicates that, regardless of the substantial schematization, the calculation method that was presented expresses correctly the main features of ice-edge dynamics. More experimental and theoretical investigations are required with a view to refining this method.

BIBLIOGRAPHY

1. AL'TBERG, V. Ya. Frazil. Moscow, GONTI. 1939.
2. ANISIMOVA, E. P. and A. A. PIVOVAROV. Calculation of the Coefficients of Turbulent Vertical Exchange in Seas and Storage Lakes. — Meteorologiya i Gidrologiya, No. 2. 1966.
3. BERLYAND, M. E. Forecasting and Regulating Thermal Conditions of the Marine Surface Layer. Leningrad, Gidrometizdat. 1956.
4. BIBIKOV, D. N. The Growth Rate of Ice Crystals in Water. — In: Ledotermicheskie problemy v gidroenergetike. Moscow, Gosenergoizdat. 1954.
5. BIBIKOV, D. N. The Problem of the Number of Ice Crystals in Supercooled Water. — DAN SSSR, Vol. 109, No. 6. 1956.
6. BIBIKOV, D. N. and N. N. PETRUNICHEV. Ice Troubles in Hydropower Stations. Moscow, Gosenergoizdat. 1956.
7. BOGUSLAVSKII, S. G. Absorption of Solar Radiation in the Sea and its Direct Effect on the Change in Water Temperature. — Trudy MGI AN SSSR, 8. 1956.
8. BOGUSLAVSKII, S. G. Vertical Turbulent Exchange in the Surface Layer of the Sea. — Trudy MGI AN SSSR, 13. 1958.
9. BRASLAVSKII, A. P. and Z. A. VIKULOVA. Average Long-Term Evaporation from the Surface of Storage Lakes. Leningrad, Gidrometizdat. 1954.
10. BUDYKO, M. I. The Heat Balance of the Earth's Surface. Leningrad, Gidrometizdat. 1956.
11. BUKINA, L. A. Laboratory Methods of Investigating Growth Rates of Ice Crystals in Water. — Izvestiya AN SSSR, Seriya Geofiziki, No. 6. 1961.
12. BUKINA, L. A. The Growth Rate of Ice Crystals in Water. — Izvestiya AN SSSR, Seriya Geofiziki, No. 12. 1962.
13. BUKINA, L. A. The Temperature Dependence of the Thickness-to-Diameter Ratio of Disk-Shaped Ice Crystals in Water. — Izvestiya AN SSSR, Seriya Geofiziki, No. 1. 1963.
14. BUKINA, L. A. The Coefficient of Heat Transfer of Disk-Shaped Ice Crystals in Water. — Izvestiya AN SSSR, Seriya Geofiziki, No. 8. 1963.

14a. BUKINA, L. A. Size Distribution of Ice Crystals in a Turbulent Water Flow. — Izvestiya AN SSSR, Seriya Geofiziki, No. 1. 1967.

15. BYDIN, F. I. Investigation of the Growth of Ice under Natural Conditions. — Izvestiya NIIG, Vol. 4. 1932.
16. VARTAZAROV, V. Ya. The Ice Regime of Armenian Rivers. — Izvestiya AN ArmSSR, No. 8. 1946.
17. VASYUKOVA, N. G. The Coefficient of Turbulent Thermal Conductivity in the Sea of Japan. — Izvestiya AN SSSR, Seriya Geofiziki, No. 9. 1963.
18. VERESHCHAGIN, G. Yu. Modern Methods of Forecasting the Thermal Conditions of Lakes. — Izvestiya AN SSSR, Seriya Geografii i Geofiziki, No. 3. 1941.
19. VOSKANYAN, A. G., A. A. PIVOVAROV, and G. G. KHUNDZHUA. The Diurnal Course of Temperature and Turbulent Exchange in the Heating of the Surface Layer of the Sea. — Izvestiya AN SSSR, Fizika Atmosfery i Okeana, Vol. 3, No. 11. 1967.
20. VOSKANYAN, A. G., A. A. PIVOVAROV, and G. G. KHUNDZHUA. Experimental Investigations of the Thermal Conditions and Turbulent Heat Exchange in the Surface Layer of the Sea. — Okeanologiya, Vol. 10, No. 4. 1970.

21. GEZENTSVEI, A. N. The Effect of the Bottom on the Temperature Distribution in a Water Body. — Trudy IO AN SSSR, Vol. 4. 1949.

22. GOTLIB, Ya. L., E. E. ZAIMIN, F. F. RAZZORENOV, and B. S. TSEITLIN. Thermal Conditions in the Ice Period on the Angara. Leningrad, Gidrometizdat. 1964.

23. DAVYDOV, V. K. The Thermal Conditions of Lake Sevan. — Materialy po issledovaniyu ozera Sevan. Leningrad, Gidrometizdat. 1933.

24. DOBROKLONSKII, S. V. The Diurnal Course of the Temperature of the Surface Layer of the Sea and of Heat Fluxes at the Sea—Atmosphere Interface. — DAN SSSR, Vol. 65, No. 4. 1944.

25. EVSTIFEEV, A. M. Regulation of Slush Ice Flow in Hydropower Stations. Moscow, Gosenergoizdat. 1958.

26. EFIMOV, V. V. and A. A. SIZOV. Experimental Investigation of the Wind Speed above Waves. — Izvestiya AN SSSR, Fizika Atmosfery i Okeana, Vol. 5, No. 9. 1969.

27. ZHUKOV, L. A. Approximate Calculation of Changes in Temperature and Salinity in the Active Layer of the Sea and their Effect on Currents. — Trudy Okeanograficheskoi komissii, Vol. II. 1961.

28. ZILITINKEVICH, S. S. The Effect of Humidity Stratification on Hydrostatic Stability. — Izvestiya AN SSSR, Fizika Atmosfery i Okeana, Vol. 2, No. 10. 1966.

29. ZILITINKEVICH, S. S. The Dynamics of the Atmospheric Boundary Layer. Leningrad, Gidrometizdat. 1970.

30. ZILITINKEVICH, S. S. and D. V. CHALIKOV. Determination of Universal Wind Speed and Temperature Profiles in the Surface Layer. — Izvestiya AN SSSR, Fizika Atmosfery i Okeana, Vol. 5, No. 9. 1968.

31. ZAIKOV, B. D. Chapters on Limnology. Leningrad, Gidrometeoizdat. 1955.

32. IVANOV-FRANTSKEVICH, G. N. Some Problems of Averaging Balance Equations. — Trudy IO AN SSSR, Vol. 60. 1958.

33. IVANOVA, Z. S. Calculation of the Coefficient of Vertical Turbulent Exchange for Different Seas. — Trudy MGI AN SSSR, Vol. 13. 1958.

34. IVANOVA, Z. S. The Coefficient of Turbulent Exchange in the Surface Layer of the Black Sea. — Trudy MGI AN SSSR, Vol. 13. 1958.

35. IVANOVA, Z. S. The Effect of Changes in the Coefficient of Turbulent Exchange on the Vertical Propagation of Temperature Waves in the Sea. — Trudy MGI AN SSSR, Vol. 13. 1958.

36. KAGAN, B. A. The Theory of Calculating the Temperature of the Active Layer of the Sea. — Trudy GGO, No. 107. 1961.

37. KITAIGORODSKII, S. A. The Physics of Air—Sea Interaction. Israel Program for Scientific Translations, Cat. No. 60108. Jerusalem. 1973.

37a. KIRILLOVA, T. V. The Radiation Balance of Lakes and Storage Lakes. Leningrad, Gidrometizdat. 1970.

38. KOLESNIKOV, A. G. Calculation of the Diurnal March of Sea—Surface Temperature. — DAN SSSR, Vol. 57, No. 2. 1947.

39. KOLESNIKOV, A. G. The Winter March of the Water Temperature in a Storage Lake. — DAN SSSR, Vol. 92, No. 1. 1953.

40. KOLESNIKOV, A. G. The Calculation of the Temperature in an Ice-Covered Water Body. — In: Ledotermicheskie voprosy v gidroenergetike. Leningrad, Gidrometizdat. 1954.

41. KOLESNIKOV, A. G. Calculation of the Diurnal Course of the Temperature of the Sea by the Heat Balance at its Surface. — Izvestiya AN SSSR, Seriya Geofiziki, No. 2. 1954.

42. KOLESNIKOV, A. G. Some Results of the Direct Determination of the Vertical Turbulent Exchange in the Sea. — In: Nekotorye problemy i rezul'taty okeanologicheskikh issledovanii. Izdatel'stvo AN SSSR. 1959.

43. KOLESNIKOV, A. G., S. G. BOGUSLAVSKII, and Z. S. IVANOVA. The Effect of Stability on the Intensity of Vertical Transfer in the Atlantic Ocean. — Okeanologiya, No. 4. 1959.

44. KOLESNIKOV, A. G. and V. I. BELYAEV. Calculation of the Process of Crystallization of Supercooled Water under Conditions of Turbulent Mixing. — Izvestiya AN SSSR, Seriya Geofiziki, No. 6. 1956.
45. KOLESNIKOV, A. G. and A. A. PIVOVAROV. Calculation of Fall Cooling of Storage Lakes. — DAN SSSR, Vol. 93, No. 6. 1953.
46. KOLESNIKOV, A. G. and A. A. PIVOVAROV. Calculation of the Diurnal March of the Sea Temperature from the Total Radiation and Air Temperature. — DAN SSSR, Vol. 102, No. 2. 1955.
47. KOLESNIKOV, A. G. and A. A. PIVOVAROV. The Possibility of Calculating the Resultant Heat Balance at the Surface of Storage Lakes from the Air Temperature. — Izvestiya AN SSSR, Seriya Geofiziki, No. 2. 1956.
48. KOLESNIKOV, A. G. and A. A. PIVOVAROV. Calculation of the Cooling Rate According to River Length. — Trudy III Vsesoyuznogo s"ezda, Vol. 3. Leningrad, Gidrometizdat. 1958.
49. KOLESNIKOV, A. G. and A. A. PIVOVAROV. Method of Calculating the Water Temperature for the Period of Fall Cooling of Storage Lakes. — Vestnik Moskovskogo universiteta, Series 3, No. 2. 1960.
50. KOLESNIKOV, A. G. and A. A. SPERANSKAYA. Diurnal Course of the Water Temperature and Speed of Thawing of the Ice Cover from Below in Storage Lakes. — Izvestiya AN SSSR, Seriya Geofiziki, No. 12. 1958.
51. KONDRAT'EV, K. Ya. The Radiant Energy of the Sun. Leningrad, Gidrometizdat. 1954.
52. KONDRAT'EV, K. Ya. Radiant Heat Exchange in the Atmosphere. Leningrad, Gidrometizdat. 1956.
53. KONDRAT'EV, K. Ya. Actinometry. Leningrad, Gidrometizdat. 1965.
54. KONDRAT'EV, K. Ya. and L. A. KUDRYAVTSEVA. Albedo of the Sea Surface. — Meteorologiya i Gidrologiya, No. 3. 1955.
55. KONDRAT'EV, K. Ya. and N. E. TER-MARKARYANTS. Albedo of the Wind-Roughened Sea. — Meteorologiya i Gidrologiya, No. 8. 1953.
56. KORYTNIKOVA, N. N. Forecasts of Winter Temperatures in Water Bodies without Runoff. — Izvestiya AN SSSR, Seriya Geografii i Geofiziki, No. 6. 1940.
57. KORYTNIKOVA, N. N. Some Methods of Calculating the Thermal Conditions of Lakes and Rivers. — Izvestiya AN SSSR, Seriya Geografii i Geofiziki, No. 3. 1941.
58. KRITSKII, S. N., M. F. MENKEL', and K. I. ROSSINSKII. Winter Thermal Conditions of Storage Lakes, Rivers, and Canals. Moscow, Gosenergoizdat. 1947.
59. LAIKHTMAN, D. L. Physics of the Atmospheric Boundary Layer. Leningrad, Gidrometizdat. 1970.
60. LINEIKIN, P. S. The Theory of Calculating the Temperature During Cooling of the Sea. — Trudy GOIN, No. 21 (33). Leningrad. 1952.
61. MARYUTIN, T. P. Forecasts of Ice Thickness in Arkhangelsk. — Trudy NIU GUGMS, Series 5, No. 12. 1946.
62. MAKKAVEEV, V. M. The Theory of Mixing Processes in the Turbulent Motion of Free Flows and Problems of the Winter Conditions on Rivers. — Izvestiya GGI, No. 5. 1931.
63. MONIN, A. S. and A. M. YAGLOM. Statistical Hydromechanics. Moscow, "Nauka." 1965.
64. MULLAMAA, Yu.-A.R. Atlas of the Optical Characteristics of the Wind-Roughened Sea Surface. — Tartu, Izdatel'stvo AN ESSR. 1964.
65. PANTELEEV, N. A. Investigation of the Turbulence in the Surface Water Layer in the Antarctic Sector of the Indian and Pacific Oceans. — Trudy Okeanograficheskoi komissii, Vol. 10, No. 1. 1960.
66. PEKHOVICH, A. I. Thermal Calculation of Deep Storage Lakes in the Ice-Free Period. — Gidrotekhnicheskoe Stroitel'stvo, No. 11. 1959.
67. PIVOVAROV, A. A. Determination of the Coefficient of Vertical Turbulent Thermal Conductivity in the Sea. — Trudy MGI AN SSSR, Vol. 4. 1954.

68. PIVOVAROV, A. A. Calculation of the Course of the Water Temperature of Storage Lakes in Winter. — DAN SSSR, Vol. 94, No. 6. 1954.

69. PIVOVAROV, A. A. Method of Forecasting the Winter Course of the Vertically Averaged Water Temperature in Storage Lakes. — Trudy III Vsesoyuznogo Gidrologicheskogo s"ezda, Vol. 4. Leningrad, Gidrometizdat. 1959.

70. PIVOVAROV, A. A. The Effect of Solar Radiation Penetrating into the Sea on the Formation of the Water Temperature. — Okeanologiya, No. 2. 1963.

71. PIVOVAROV, A. A. Forecast of the Vertically Averaged Sub-Ice Water Temperatures of Lakes with Runoff. — Vestnik Moskovskogo universiteta, Series 3, No. 4. 1966.

72. PIVOVAROV, A. A. The Diurnal Course of the Temperature in Surface and Marine Surface Layers. — Izvestiya AN SSSR, Fizika Atmosfery i Okeana, Vol. 4, No. 1. 1968.

73. PIVOVAROV, A. A., E. P. ANISIMOVA, and A. N. ERIKOVA. Diurnal Course of the Albedo and of the Solar Radiation Penetrating into the Sea. — Izvestiya AN SSSR, Fizika Atmosfery i Okeana, Vol. 1, No. 11. 1955.

74. PIVOVAROV, A. A., E. P. ANISIMOVA, and L. A. BUKINA. The Diurnal Course of the Water Temperature for Vertically Varying Turbulent Exchange and Volume Absorption of Solar Radiation. — Vestnik Moskovskogo universiteta, Series 3, No. 2. 1968.

75. PIVOVAROV, A. A. and V. S. LAVORKO. Vertical Attenuation of Solar Radiation in the Sea. — Vestnik Moskovskogo universiteta, Series 3, No. 6. 1960.

76. PIVOVAROV, A. A. and V. S. LAVORKO. The Diurnal Course of the Components of Solar Radiation and Sea Albedo. — Meteorologiya i Gidrologiya, No. 1. 1961.

77. PIOTROVICH, V. V. Formation and Thawing of Ice on Storage Lakes and Calculation of the Times of Freeze-up and Thawing of Ice. Leningrad, Gidrometizdat. 1958.

78. PROTASOV, S. N. The Diurnal Course of the Temperature in the Surface and Marine Surface Layers with Variable Coefficients of Turbulent Heat Exchange. — Vestnik Moskovskogo universiteta, Series 3, No. 2. 1968.

79. ROLL, H. U. Physics of the Marine Atmosphere. New York—London, Academic Press. 1965.

80. ROSOLIMO, L. L. Temperature Conditions in Lake Baikal. — Trudy Baikalskoi limnologicheskoi stantsii AN SSSR, Vol. 16. 1957.

81. RUTKOVSKII, V. I. Temperature Conditions of the Rybinsk Reservoir. — Trudy instituta biologii vodokhranilishch, No. 5. 1963.

82. SAMOILENKO, V. S. Formation of the Temperature Regime of Seas. Leningrad, Gidrometizdat. 1959.

83. SPERANSKAYA, A. A. Investigation of the Turbulence of Storage Lakes with Low Runoff. — Trudy III Vsesoyuznogo Gidrologicheskogo s"ezda, Vol. 4. Leningrad, Gidrometizdat. 1959.

84. TER-MARKARYANTS, N. E. Reflection of Radiation by the Sea in the Presence of Waves. — Trudy GGO, No. 68. 1957.

85. TER-MARKARYANTS, N. E. Mean Diurnal Values of Sea Albedo.—Trudy GGO, No. 100. 1959.

86. TIMOFEEV, M. P. The Meteorological Regime of Lakes and Rivers. Leningrad, Gidrometizdat. 1963.

87. HINZE, J. O. Turbulence: An Introduction to its Mechanism and Theory. New York, McGraw Hill. 1959.

88. CHIZHOV, G. B. The Problem of Supercooling and Crystallization of Water under Different Conditions. — Meteorologiya i Gidrologiya, No. 4. 1940.

89. SHVETS, M. E. Approximate Theory of Ice Buildup. — Meteorologiya i Gidrologiya, No. 5. 1949.

90. SHTOKMAN, V. B. Vertical Propagation of Thermal Waves in the Sea and Indirect Methods of Determining the Coefficients of Thermal Conductivity. — Trudy IO AN SSSR, Vol. 1. 1946.

91. SHULEIKIN, V. V. Physics of the Sea. Moscow, Izdatel'stvo AN SSSR. 1968.
92. SHULYAKOVSKII, L. G. The Appearance of Ice and the Onset of Freezing on Rivers, Lakes, and Storage Lakes. Leningrad, Gidrometizdat. 1960.
93. ARAKAWA, K. The Growth of Ice Crystals in Water. — J. Glaciology, Vol. 2. 1955.
94. ARAKAWA, K. Experimental Studies of Freezing of Water. — International Union of Geodesy and Geophysics. 1954.
95. BURT, W. Albedo over Wind-Roughened Water. — J. Met., Vol. 7, No. 4. 1954.
96. COX, C. and W. MUNK. Some Problems in Optical Oceanography. — J. Mar. Res., Vol. 14, No. 1. 1955.
97. DEVIK, O. Ice Formation in Lakes and Rivers. — Intern. Union of Geodesy and Geophysics, Inst. Assocn. Sci. Hydrology, Trans., Oslo, Vol. 2. 1948.
98. DEVIK, O. Thermische und dynamische Bedingungen der Eisbildung in Wasserläufen. — Geophys. Publ. 1932.
99. EMDEN, R. Zur Temperatur der Seen. — Helvetica Physica Acta, Vol. 13. 1940.
100. ERTEL, H. Theorie der thermischen Sprungschicht in Seen. — Acta Hydrophysica, Vol. 1, No. 4. 1954.
101. FJELDSTAD, J. E. Wärmeleitung im Meer. — Geophys. Publ., Vol. 10, No. 7. 1933.
102. KUMAI, M. and K. ITAGAKI. Cinematographic Study of Ice Crystal Formation in Water. — J. of Faculty of Science, Hokkaido University, Vol. 4, Series 2. 1953.
103. SCHMITZ, H. P. Über die Abkühlung von Binnenseen. — Acta hydrophysica, Berlin, Vol. 1, No. 1. 1953.
104. ROSSINSKII, K. I. The Temperature Conditions of Deep Water Bodies. — Trudy III Vsesoyuznogo gidrologicheskogo s"ezda, Vol. IV. Leningrad, Gidrometeoizdat. 1958.

EXPLANATORY LIST OF ABBREVIATIONS OF USSR INSTITUTIONS APPEARING IN THIS TEXT

Abbreviation	Full name (transliterated)	Translation
AN ArmSSR	Akademiya Nauk Armyanskoi SSR	Academy of Sciences of the Armenian SSR
DAN SSSR	Doklady Akademii Nauk SSSR	Proceedings of the Academy of Sciences, USSR
GGI	Gosudarstvennyi Gidrologicheskii Institut	State Hydrological Institute
GGO	Glavnaya Geofizicheskaya Observatoriya im. A. I. Voeikova	Voeikov Main Geophysical Observatory
GOIN	Gosudarstvennyi Okeanograficheskii Institut	State Institute of Oceanography
GONTI	Gosudarstvennoe Ob"edinennoe Nauchno-Tekhnicheskoe Izdatel'stvo	State Joint Scientific and Technical Publishing House
GUGMS	Glavnoe Upravlenie Gidrometeorologicheskoi Sluzhby	Main Administration of the Hydrometeorological Service
IO AN SSSR	Institut Okeanologii Akademii Nauk SSSR	Institute of Oceanology of the Academy of Sciences, USSR
MGI AN SSSR	Morskoi Gidrofizicheskii Institut (Akademii Nauk SSSR)	Marine Hydrophysical Institute (of the Academy of Sciences, USSR)
NIIG	Nauchno-Issledovatel'skii Institut Gidrotekhniki	Research Institute of Hydraulic Engineering

SUBJECT INDEX